OPHIOLATREIA

An Account of the Rites and Mysteries Connected with the Origin, Rise, and Development of Serpent Worship in various Parts of the World, Enriched with Interesting Traditions, and A Full Description of the Celebrated Serpent Mounds & Temples, Forming An Exposition of One of the Phasks of Phallic, or Sex Worship.

Hargrave Jennings

ISBN 1-56459-944-2

PREFACE.

—

OUR words by way of preface and introduction need be but few. The following volume forms a companion to one already issued bearing the title "Phallism." That work, though complete in itself, meets in this a further elucidation of its subject, since, in the opinion of many, Ophiolatreia, the worship of the Serpent, is of Phallic origin. Such a view, and others of a contrary nature, have been honestly set forth, and the best and most trustworthy authorities have been consulted for history, arguments, and illustrations by which they may be understood. No attempt has been made to insist upon any one method of interpretation as undoubtedly correct, but simple facts have been stated, and the reader has been left to form his own independent judgment.

CONTENTS.

OPHIOLATREIA.

CHAPTER I.

Ophiolatreia an extraordinary subject—Of mysterious origin—Of universal prevalence — The serpent a common symbol in mythology—Serpent-worship natural but irrational—Bacchic orgies—Olympias, mother of Alexander, and the Serpent emblem—Thermutis, the Sacred Serpent—Asps—Saturn and his children—Sacrifices at altar of Saturn — Abaddon — Ritual of Zoroaster—Theology of Ophion—The Cuthites—The Othiogeneis—The Ophiomans—Greek Traditions—Cecrops—Various Serpent worshippers.

OPHIOLATREIA, the worship of the serpent, next to the adoration of the phallus, is one of the most remarkable, and, at first sight, unaccountable forms of religion the world has ever known. Until the true source from whence it sprang can be reached and understood, its nature will remain as mysterious as its universality, for what man could see in an object so repulsive and forbidding in its habits as this reptile, to render worship to, is one of the most difficult of problems to find a solution to. There is hardly a country of the ancient world, however, where it cannot be traced, pervading every known system of mythology, and leaving proofs of its existence and extent in the shape of monuments, temples, and earthworks of the most elaborate and curious character. Babylon, Persia, Hindostan, Ceylon, China, Japan, Burmah, Java, Arabia, Syria, Asia Minor, Egypt, Ethiopia, Greece, Italy, Northern and Western Europe, Mexico, Peru, America—all yield abundant testimony to the same effect, and point to the common origin of Pagan systems wherever found. Whether the worship was the result of fear or respect is a question that naturally enough presents itself, and in seeking to answer it we shall be confronted with the fact that in some places, as Egypt, the symbol was that of a good demon, while in India, Scandinavia, and Mexico, it was that of an evil one. It has been remarked that in the warmer regions of the globe, where this creature is the most formidable enemy which man can encounter, the serpent should be considered the mythological attendant of an evil being is not surprising, but that in the frozen or temperate regions of the earth, where he dwindles into the insignificance of a reptile without power to create alarm, he should be regarded in the same appalling character, is a fact which cannot be accounted for by natural causes. Uniformity of tradition can alone satisfactorily explain uniformity of super-stition, where local circumstances are so discordant.

" The serpent is the symbol which most generally enters into the mythology of the world. It may in different countries admit among its fellow-satellites of Satan the most venomous or the most terrible of the animals in each country, but it preserves its own constancy, as the only invariable object of superstitious terror throughout the habitable world. 'Wherever the Devil reigned,' remarks Stillingfleet, 'the serpent was held in some peculiar veneration.' The universality of this singular and irrational, yet natural, superstition it is now proposed to show. *Irrational*, for there is nothing in common between deity and a reptile, to suggest the notion of Serpent-worship; and *natural*, because, allowing the truth of the events in Paradise, every probability is in favour of such a superstition springing up."*

It may seem extraordinary that the worship of the serpent should ever have been introduced into the world, and it must appear still more remarkable that it should almost universally have prevailed. As mankind are said to have been ruined through the influence of this being, we could little expect that it would, of all other objects, have been adopted as the most sacred

* Deane.

and salutary symbol, and rendered the chief object of adoration. Yet so we find it to have been, for in most of the ancient rites there is some allusion to it. In the orgies of Bacchus, the persons who took part in the ceremonies used to carry serpents in their hands, and with horrid screams call upon "Eva, Eva." They were often crowned with serpents while still making the same frantic exclamation. One part of the mysterious rites of Jupiter Sabazius was to let a snake slip down the bosom of the person to be initiated, which was taken out below. These ceremonies, and this symbolic worship, are said to have begun among the Magi, who were the sons of Chus, and by them they were propagated in various parts. Epiphanius thinks that the invocation "Eva, Eva," related to the great mother of mankind, who was deceived by the serpent, and Clemens of Alexandria is of the same opinion. Others, however, think that Eva was the same as Eph, Epha, Opha, which the Greeks rendered Ophis, and by it denoted a serpent. Clemens acknowledges that the term Eva, properly aspirated, had such a signification.

Olympias, the mother of Alexander, was very fond of these orgies, in which the serpent was introduced. Plutarch mentions that rites of this sort were practised by the Edonian women near Mount Hæmus in Thrace, and carried on to a degree of madness. Olympias copied them closely in all their frantic manœuvres. She used to be followed with many attendants, who had each a thyrsus with serpents twined round it. They had also snakes in their hair, and in the chaplets which they wore, so that they made a most fearful appearance. Their cries also were very shocking, and the whole was attended with a continual repetition of the words, Evoe, Saboe, Hues Attes, Attes Hues, which were titles of the god Dionusus. He was peculiarly named Hues, and his priests were the Hyades and Hyautes. He was likewise styled Evas.

In Egypt was a serpent named Thermuthis, which was looked upon as very sacred; and the natives are said to have made use of it as a royal tiara, with which they ornamented the statues of Isis. We learn from Diodorus Siculus that the kings of Egypt wore high bonnets, which terminated in a round ball, and the whole was surrounded with figures of asps. The priests, likewise, upon their bonnets had the representation of serpents. The ancients had a notion that when Saturn devoured his own children, his wife Ops deceived him by substituting a large stone in lieu of one of his sons, which stone was called Abadir. But Ops and Opis, represented here as a feminine, was the serpent deity, and Abadir is the same personage under a different denomination. Abadir seems to be a variation of Ob-Adur, and signifies the serpent god Orus. One of these stones, which Saturn was supposed to have swallowed instead of a child, stood, according to Pausanias, at Delphi. It was esteemed very sacred, and used to have libations of wine poured upon it daily; and upon festivals was otherwise honoured. The purport of the above was probably this: it was for a long time a custom to offer children at the altar of Saturn; but in process of time they removed it, and in its room erected a stone pillar, before which they made their vows, and offered sacrifices of another nature. This stone which they thus substituted was called Ab-Adar, from the deity represented by it. The term Ab generally signifies a father, but in this instance it certainly relates to a serpent, which was indifferently styled Ab, Aub, and Ob. Some regard Abadon, or, as it is mentioned in the Book of the Revelation, Abaddon, to have been the name of the same Ophite god, with whose worship the world had been so long infected. He is termed Abaddon, the angel of the bottomless pit—the prince of darkness. In another place he is described as the dragon, that old serpent, which is the devil, and Satan. Hence the learned

Heinsius is supposed to be right in the opinion which he has given upon this passage, when he makes Abaddon the same as the serpent Pytho.

It is said that in the ritual of Zoroaster the great expanse of the heavens, and even nature itself, was described under the symbol of a serpent.* The like was mentioned in the Octateuch of Ostanes; and moreover, in Persia and in other parts of the East they erected temples to the serpent tribe, and held festivals to their honour, esteeming them *the supreme of all Gods, and the superintendents of the whole world*. The worship began among the people of Chaldea. They built the city Opis upon the Tigris, and were greatly addicted to divination and to the worship of the serpent. From Chaldea the worship passed into Egypt, where the serpent deity was called Canoph, Caneph, and C'neph. It had also the name of Ob, or Oub, and was the same as the Basilicus, or Royal Serpent; the same also as the Thermuthis, and in like manner was made use of by way of ornament to the statues of their Gods. The chief Deity of Egypt is said to have been Vulcan, who was also styled Opas, as we learn from Cicero. He was the same as Osiris, the Sun; and hence was often called Ob-El, or Pytho Sol; and there were pillars sacred to him, with curious hieroglyphical inscriptions, which had the same name. They were very lofty, and narrow in comparison of their length; hence among the Greeks, who copied from the Egyptians, everything gradually tapering to a point was styled Obelos, and Obeliscus. Ophel (Oph-El) was a name of the same purport, and many sacred mounds, or Tapha, were thus denominated from the serpent Deity, to whom they were sacred.

Sanchoniathon makes mention of a history which he once wrote upon the worship of the serpent. The title of this work, according to Eusebius, was Ethothion, or Ethothia. Another treatise upon the same subject was written by Pherecydes Tyrus,

* Eusebius.

which was probably a copy of the former; for he is said to have composed it from some previous accounts of the Phœnicians. The title of his book was the Theology of Ophion, styled Ophioneus, and his worshippers were called Ophionidæ. Thoth and Athoth were certainly titles of the Deity in the Gentile world; and the book of Sanchoniathon might very possibly have been from hence named Ethothion, or more truly, Athothion. But, from the subject upon which it was written, as well as from the treatise of Pherecydes, we have reason to think that Athothion, or Ethothion, was a mistake for Ath-Ophion, a title which more immediately related to that worship of which the writer treated. Ath was a sacred title, as we have shewn, and we imagine that this dissertation did not barely relate to the serpentine Deity, but contained accounts of his votaries, the Ophitæ, the principal of which were the sons of Chus. The worship of the serpent began among them, and they were from thence denominated Ethiopians, and Aithopians, which the Greeks render Aithiopes. They did not receive this name from their complexion, as has sometimes been surmised, for the branch of Phut and the Luhim, were probably of a deeper dye; but they were most likely so called from Ath-Ope, and Ath-Opis, the God which they worshipped. This may be shewn from Pliny. He says that the country Ethiopia (and consequently the people), had the name of Æthiop, from a personage who was a Deity—*ab Æthiope Vulcani filio*. The Æthiopes brought these rites into Greece, and called the island where they first established them Ellopia, *Solis Serpentis insula*. It was the same as Eubœa, a name of the like purport, in which island was a region named Ethiopium. Eubœa is properly Oub-Aia, and signifies the Serpent Island. The same worship prevailed among the Hyperboreans, as we may judge from the names of the sacred women who used to come annually to Delos; they were priestesses of the Tauric Goddess.

Hercules was esteemed the chief God, the same as Chronus, and was said to have produced the Mundane egg. He was represented in the Orphic theology under the mixed symbol of a lion and a serpent, and sometimes of a serpent only.

The Cuthites, under the title of Heliadæ, having settled at Rhodes, as they were Hivites, or Ophites, the island was in consequence named Ophiusa. There was likewise a tradition that it had once swarmed with serpents. (Bochart says the island is said to have been named Rhodus from *Rhad*, a Syriac word for a serpent). The like notion prevailed almost in every place where they settled. They came under the more general titles of Leleges and Pelasgi; but more particularly of Elopians, Europians, Oropians, Asopians, Inopians, Ophionians, and Æthiopes, as appears from the names which they bequeathed; and in most places where they resided there were handed down traditions which alluded to their original title of Ophites. In Phrygia, and upon the Hellespont, whither they sent out colonies very early, was a people styled the Ophiogeneis, or the serpent breed, who were said to retain an affinity and correspondence with serpents; and a notion prevailed that some hero, who had conducted them, was changed from a serpent to a man. In Colchis was a river Ophis, and there was another of the same name in Arcadia. It was so named from a body of people who settled upon its banks, and were said to have been conducted by a serpent.

It is said these reptiles are seldom found in islands, but that Tenos, one of the Cyclades, was supposed to have once swarmed with them.*

Thucydides mentions a people of Ætotia, called Ophionians; and the temple of Apollo at Petara, in Lycia, seems to have had its first institution from a priestess of the same name. The island of Cyprus was called Ophiusa, and Ophiodes, from the

* Aristoph.

serpents with which it was supposed to have abounded. Of what species they were is nowhere mentioned, excepting only that about Paphos there was said to have been a kind of serpent with two legs. By this is meant the Ophite race, who came from Egypt, and from Syria, and got footing in this island. They settled also in Crete, where they increased greatly in numbers; so that Minos was said by an unseemly allegory, *ophcis ouresai, serpentes, minxisse*. The island Seriphus was one vast rock, by the Romans called *saxum seriphium*, and made use of as a large kind of prison for banished persons. It is represented as having once abounded with serpents, and it is styled by Virgil, *serpentifera*, as the passage is corrected by Scaliger.

It is said by the Greeks that Medusa's head was brought by Perseus; by this is meant the serpent Deity, whose worship was here introduced by people called Peresians. Medusa's head denoted divine wisdom, and the island was sacred to the serpent, as is apparent from its name. The Athenians were esteemed *Serpentiginæ*, and they had a tradition that the chief guardian of their Acropolis was a serpent.

It is reported of the goddess Ceres that she placed a dragon for a guardian to her temple at Eleusis, and appointed another to attend upon Erectheus. Ægeus of Athens, according to Androtion, was of the serpent breed, and the first king of the country is said to have been a dragon. Others make Cecrops the first who reigned. He is said to have been of a two-fold nature, being formed with the body of a man blended with that of a serpent. Diodorus says that this was a circumstance deemed by the Athenians inexplicable; yet he labours to explain it by representing Cecrops as half a man and half a brute, because he had been of two different communities. Eustathius likewise tries to solve it nearly upon the same principles, and with the like success. Some have said of Cecrops that he underwent a metamorphosis, being changed from a serpent to a man. By this was meant, according to Eustathius, that Cecrops by coming into Hellas divested himself of all the rudeness and barbarity of his country, and became more civilised and human. This is declared by some to be too high a compliment to be paid to Greece in its infant state, and detracts greatly from the character of the Egyptians. The learned Marsham therefore animadverts with great justice, " it is more probable that he introduced into Greece the urbanity of his own country, than that he was beholden to Greece for anything from thence." In respect to the mixed character of this personage, we may easily account for it. Cecrops was certainly a title of the Deity, who was worshipped under this emblem. Something of the like nature was mentioned of Triptolemus and Ericthonius, and the like has been said of Hercules. The natives of Thebes in Bœotia, like the Athenians, esteemed themselves of the serpent race. The Lacedæmonians likewise referred themselves to the same original. Their city is said of old to have swarmed with serpents. The same is said of the city Amyelæ in Italy, which was of Spartan origin. They came hither in such abundance that it was abandoned by the inhabitants. Argos was infested in the same manner till Apis came from Egypt and settled in that city. He was a prophet, the reputed son of Apollo, and a person of great skill and sagacity, and to him they attributed the blessing of having their country freed from this evil. Thus the Argives gave the credit to this imaginary personage of clearing their land of this grievance, but the brood came from the very quarter from whence Apis was supposed to have arrived. They were certainly Hivites from Egypt, and the same story is told of that country. It is represented as having been of old over-run with serpents, and almost depopulated through their numbers. Diodorus Siculus seems to understand this literally, but a region that was annually overflowed, and that too for so long a season, could not well be liable to such a calamity. They were serpents of another nature with which it was thus infested, and the history relates to the Cuthites, the original Ophitæ, who for a long time possessed that country. They passed from Egypt to Syria, and to the Euphrates, and mention is made of a particular breed of serpents upon that river, which were harmless to the natives but fatal to anybody else. This can hardly be taken literally; for whatever may be the wisdom of the serpent it cannot be sufficient to make these distinctions. These serpents were of the same nature as the birds of Diomedes, and the dogs in the temple of Vulcan; and the histories relate to Ophite priests, who used to spare their own people and sacrifice strangers, a custom which prevailed at one time in most parts of the world. The Cuthite priests are said to have been very learned; and, as they were Ophites, whoever had the advantage of their information was said to have been instructed by serpents.

As the worship of the serpent was of old so prevalent, many places, as well as people, from thence received their names. Those who settled in Campania were called Opici, which some would have changed to Ophici, because they were denominated from serpents. They are in reality both names of the same purport, and denote the origin of the people.

We meet with places called Opis, Ophis, Ophitæa, Ophionia, Ophioessa, Ophiodes, and Ophiusa. This last was an ancient name by which, according to Stephanus, the islands Rhodes, Cynthus, Besbicus, Tenos, and the whole continent of Africa, were distinguished. There were also cities so called. Add to these places denominated Oboth, Obona, and reversed, Onoba, from Ob, which was of the same purport.

lemens Alexandrinus says that the term Eva signified a
nt if pronounced with a proper aspirate, and Epiphanius
the same thing.   We find that there were places of this
. There was a city Eva in Arcadia, and another in Mace-
. There was also a mountain Eva, or Evan, taken notice of
ausanias, between which and Ithome lay the city Messene.
entions also an Eva in Argolis, and speaks of it as a large
.   Another name for a serpent, which we have not yet
ed, was Patan, or Pitan.   Many places in different parts
denominated from this term.   Among others was a city in
nia, and another in Mysia, which Stephanus styles a city of
a.   They were undoubtedly so named from the worship of
erpent, Pitan, and had probably Dracontia, which were
es and devices relative to the religion which prevailed.
mentions the latter city, and has some allusions to its
nt history when he describes Medea as flying through the
om Athea to Colchis.   The city was situate upon the ruin
or Evan, which the Greeks rendered Evenus.   According
rabo it is compounded of Eva-Ain, the fountain or river of
the serpent.

t is remarkable that the Opici, who are said to have been
d from serpents, had also the name of Pitanatæ; at least,
part of that family was so called.   Pitanatæ is a term of the
purport as Opici, and relates to the votaries of Pitan, the
nt Deity, which was adored by that people.   Menelaus was
d called Pitanates, as we learn from Hesychius, and the
n of it may be known from his being a Spartan, by which
as intimated one of the Serpentigenæ, or Ophites.   Hence
as represented with a serpent for a device upon his shield.
said that a brigade, or portion of infantry, was among some
e Greeks named Pitanates, and the soldiers in consequence
must have been termed Pitanatæ, undoubtedly, because they

had the Pitan, or serpent, for their standard.   Analogous
this, among other nations there were soldiers called Draconas
In most countries the military standard was an emblem of t
Deity there worshipped.

What has already been said has thrown some light upon t
history of this primitive idolatry, and we have shewn th
wherever any of these Ophite colonies settled, they left behi
from their rites and institutions, as well as from the names whi
they bequeathed to places, ample memorials, by which they m
be clearly traced out.

CHAPTER II.

Supposed Phallic origin of Serpent-worship —The Idea of Life—
Adoration of the Principle of Generation—The Serpent as a Sym-
bol of the Phallus—Phallic Worship at Benares—The Serpent and
Mahadeo—Festival of the " Nag pauchami"—Snakes and Women
—Traces of Phallic Worship in the Kumaon Rock-markings—The
Northern Bulb Stones — Professor Stephens on the Snake as a
Symbol of the Phallus—The " Dionysiak Myth"—Brown on the
Serpent as a Phallic emblem — Mythology of the Aryan Nations—
Sir G. W. Cox and the Phallic Theory—Athenian Mythology.

SOME persons are disposed to attribute to the Serpent, as a
religious emblem, an origin decidedly phallic. Mr. C. S.
Wake takes a contrary view, and says :—" So far as I can make
out the serpent symbol has not a direct Phallic reference, nor is
its attribute of wisdom the most essential. The idea most intimately associated with this animal was that of life, not present
merely, but continued, and probably everlasting. . Thus the
snake *Bai* was figured as Guardian of the doorways of the
Egyptian Tombs which represented the mansions of heaven. A
sacred serpent would seem to have been kept in all the Egyptian.
temples, and we are told that many of the subjects, in the tombs
of the kings at Thebes in particular, show the importance it was
thought to enjoy in a future state. Crowns, formed of the Asp
or sacred *Thermuthis*, were given to sovereigns and divinities,
particularly to Isis, and these no doubt were intended to symbolise
eternal life. Isis was a goddess of life and healing and the serpent evidently belonged to her in that character, seeing that it
was the symbol also of other deities with the like attributes.
Thus, on papyri it encircles the figure of Harpocrates, who was
identified with Æsculapius ; while not only was a great serpent
kept alive in the great temple of Serapis, but on later monuments.

this god is represented by a great serpent with or without a human head. Mr. Fergusson, in accordance with his. peculiar theory as to the origin of serpent worship, thinks this superstition characterised the old Turanaian (or rather let us say Akkadian) empire of Chaldea, while tree-worship was more a characteristic of the later Assyrian Empire. This opinion is no doubt correct, and it means really that the older race had that form of faith with which the serpent was always indirectly connected — adoration of the male principle of generation, the principal phase of which was probably ancestor worship, while the latter race adored the female principle, symbolised by the sacred tree, the Assyrian 'grove.' The 'tree of life,' however, undoubtedly had reference to the male element, and we may well imagine that originally the fruit alone was treated as symbolical of the opposite element."

Mr. J. H. Rivett-Carnac, in his paper printed in the journal of the Asiatic Society of Bengal, entitled " The Snake Symbol in India," suggests that the serpent is a symbol of the phallus. He says:—" The serpent appears on the prehistoric cromlechs and menhirs of Europe, on which I believe the remains of phallic worship may be traced. What little attention I have been able to give to the serpent-symbol has been chiefly in its connection with the worship of Mahádeo or Siva, with a view to ascertain whether the worship of the snake and. that of Mahádeo or the phallus may be considered identical, and whether the presence of the serpent on the prehistoric remains of Europe can be shown to support my theory, that the markings on the cromlechs and menhirs are indeed the traces of this form of worship, carried to Europe from the East by the tribes whose remains are buried beneath the tumuli.

During my visits to Benares, the chief centre of Siva worship in India, I have always carefully searched for the snake-symbol.

On the most ordinary class of " Mahádeo," a rough stone placed on end supposed to represent the phallus, the serpent is not generally seen. But in the temples and in the better class of shrines which abound in the city and neighbourhood the snake is generally found encircling the phallus. The tail of the snake is sometimes carried down the *Yoni*, and in one case I found two snakes on a shrine thus depicted.

In the Benares bazaar I once came across a splendid metal cobra, the head erect and hood expanded, so made as to be placed around or above a stone or metal "Mahádeo." It is now in England. The attitude of the cobra when excited and the expansion of the head will suggest the reason for this snake representing Mahádeo and the phallus.

Although the presence of the snake in these models cannot be said to prove much, and although from the easy adaptability of its form the snake must always have been a favourite subject in ornament, still it will be seen that the serpent is prominent in connection with the conventional shape under which Mahádeo is worshipped at Benares and elsewhere, that it sometimes takes the place of the Linga, and that it is to be found entwined with almost every article connected with this worship."

Further on the same writer says:—" The Nág panchami or fifth day of the moon in Sawan is a great fete in the city of Nágpúr, and more than usual license is indulged in on that day. Rough pictures of snakes in all sorts of shapes and positions are sold and distributed, something after the manner of valentines. I cannot find any copies of these queer sketches, and if I could they would hardly be fit to be reproduced. Mr. J. W. Neill, the present Commissioner of Nágpúr, was good enough to send me some superior valentines of this class, and I submit them now for the inspection of the Society. It will be seen that in these paintings, some of which are not without merit either as to design or execution, no human figures are introduced. In the ones I have seen in days gone by the positions of the women with the snakes were of the most indecent description and left no doubt that, so far as the idea represented in these sketches was concerned, the cobra was regarded as the phallus. In the pictures now sent the snakes will be seen represented in congress in the well-known form of the Caduceus Esculapian rod. Then the many-headed snake, drinking from the jewelled cup, takes me back to some of the symbols of the mysteries of bygone days. The snake twisted round the tree and the second snake approaching it are suggestive of the temptation and fall. But I am not unmindful of the pitfalls from which Wilford suffered, and I quite see that it is not impossible that this picture may be held to be not strictly Hindu in its treatment. Still the tree and the serpent are on the brass models which accompany this paper, and which I have already shewn are to be purchased in the Benares Brass Bazaar of to-day—many hundreds of miles away from Nágpúr where these Valentines were drawn.

In my paper on the Kumáon Rock Markings, besides noting the resemblance between the cup markings of India and Europe, I hazarded the theory that the concentric circles and certain curious markings of what some have called the ' jew's harp ' type, so common in Europe, are traces of Phallic worship carried there by tribes whose hosts descended into India, pushed forward into the remotest corners of Europe, and, as their traces seem to suggest, found their way on to the American Continent too. Whether the markings really ever were intended to represent the Phallus and the Yoni must always remain a matter of opinion. But I have no reason to be dissatisfied with the reception with which this, to many somewhat pleasant theory, has met in some of the Antiquarian Societies of Europe.

No one who compares the stone Yonis of Benares, sent herewith, with the engravings on the first page of the work on the Rock Markings of Northumberland and Argyleshire, published privately by the Duke of Northumberland, will deny that there is an extraordinary resemblance between the conventional symbol of Siva worship of to-day and the ancient markings on the rocks, menhirs, and cromlechs of Northumberland, of Scotland, of Brittany, of Scandinavia, and other parts of Europe.

And a further examination of the forms of the cromlechs and tumuli and menhirs will suggest that the tumuli themselves were intended to indicate the symbols of the Mahádeo and Yoni, conceived in no obscene sense, but as representing regeneration, the new life, " life out of death, life everlasting," which those buried in the tumuli, facing towards the sun in its meridian, were expected to enjoy in the hereafter. Professor Stephens, the well-known Scandinavian Antiquary, writing to me recently, speaks of the symbols as follows: —" The pieces (papers) you were so good as to send me were very valuable and welcome. There can be no doubt that it is to India we have to look for the solution of many of our difficult archæological questions."

" But especially interesting is your paper on the Ancient Rock-Sculpturings. I believe that you are quite right in your views. Nay, I go further. I think that the northern Bulb-stones are explained by the same combination. I therefore send you the Swedish Archæological Journal for 1876, containing Baron Herculius' excellent dissertation on these objects. . . . You can examine the many excellent woodcuts. I look upon these things as late conventionalized abridgments of the Linga and Yoni, life out of death, life everlasting—thus a fitting ornament for the graves of the departed."

c

The author further says:—" Many who indignantly repudiate the idea of the prevalence of Phallic Worship among our remote ancestors hold that these symbols represent the snake or the sun. But admitting this, may not the snake, after all, have been but a symbol of the phallus? And the sun, the invigorating power of nature, has ever, I believe, been considered to represent the same idea, not necessarily obscene, but the great mystery of nature, the life transmitted from generation to generation, or, as Professor Stephens puts it, ' life out of death, life everlasting.' " The same idea, in fact, which, apart from any obscene conception, causes the rude Mahádeo and Yoni to be worshipped daily by hundreds of thousands of Hindus.

Brown, in his " Great Dionysiak Myth," says :—" The Serpent has six principal points of connection with Dionysos: 1—As a symbol of, and connected with, wisdom. 2—As a solar emblem. 3—As a symbol of time and eternity. 4—As an emblem of the earth, life. 5—As connected with fertilizing moisture. 6—As a phallic emblem."

Referring to the last of these, he proceeds—" The serpent being connected with the sun, the earth life and fertility must needs be also a phallic emblem, and so appropriate to the cult of Dionysos Priapos. Mr. Cox after a review of the subject, observes, ' Finally, the symbol of the Phallus suggested the form of the serpent, which thus became the emblem of life and healing. There then we have the key to that tree and serpent worship which has given rise to much ingenious speculation.' The myth of the serpent and the tree is not, I apprehend, exhausted by any merely phallic explanation, but the phallic element is certainly one of the most prominent features in it, as it might be thought any inspection of the carvings connected with the Topes of Sanchi and Amravati would show. It is hard to believe, with Mr. Fergusson, that the usefulness and beauty of trees gained them the payment of divine honours. Again, the Asherah or Grove-cult (Exod. 34, 13; 1 Kings 17, 16; Jer. 17, 2; Micah 5, 14) was essentially Phallic, Asherah being the Upright. It seems also to have been in some degree connected with that famous relic, the brazen serpent of Nehushtan (2 Kings 18, 4). Donaldson considers that the Serpent is the emblem of desire. It has also been suggested that the creature symbolised sensation generally."

The Sir G. W. Cox referred to above, in his "Mythology of Argai Nations," says:—" If there is one point more certain than another it is that wherever tree and serpent worship has been found, the cultus of the Phallos and the Ship, of the Linga and Yoni, in connection with the worship of the sun, has been found also. It is impossible to dispute the fact, and no explanation can be accepted for one part of the cultus which fails to explain the other. It is unnecessary, therefore, to analyse theories which profess to see in it the worship of the creeping brute or the wide-spreading tree. A religion based on the worship of the venomous reptile must have been a religion of terror; in the earliest glimpses which we have of it, the serpent is a symbol of life and of love. Nor is the Phallic cultus in any respect a cultus of the full-grown and branching tree. In its earliest form the symbol is every-where a mere stauros, or pole; and although this stock or rod budded in the shape of the thyrsus and the shepherd's staff, yet, even in its latest developments, the worship is confined to small bushes and shrubs and diminutive plants of a particular kind. Nor is it possible again to dispute the fact that every nation, at some stage or other of its history, has attached to this cultus precisely that meaning which the Brahman now attaches to the Linga and the Yoni. That the Jews clung to it in this special sense with vehement tenacity is the bitter complaint of the prophets; and the crucified serpent adored for its healing powers stood untouched in the Temple until it was removed and destroyed

by Hesekiah. This worship of serpents, "void of reason," con-
demned in the Wisdom of Solomon, probably survived even the
Babylonish captivity. Certainly it was adopted by the Christians
who were known as Ophites, Gnostics, and Nicolaitans. In
Athenian mythology the serpent and the tree are singularly
prominent. Kekrops, Erechtheus, and Erichthonios, are each
and all serpentine in the lower portion of their bodies. The
sacred snake of Athênê had its abode in the Akropolis, and her
olive trees secured for her the victory in her rivalry with Poseidôn.
The health-giving serpent lay at the feet of Asklêpios and snakes
were fed in his temple at Epidauros and elsewhere. That the
ideas of mere terror and death suggested by the venomous or the
crushing reptile could never have given way thus completely
before those of life, healing, and safety, is obvious enough; and
the latter ideas alone are associated with the serpent as the object
of adoration. The deadly beast always was, and has always
remained, the object of the horror and loathing which is expressed
for Ahi, the choking and throttling snake, the Vritra whom
Indra smites with his unerring lance, the dreadful Azidahaka of
the Avesta, the Zohak or Biter of modern Persian mythology, the
serpents whom Heraktes strangles in his cradle, the Python, or
Fafnir, or Grendel, or Sphinx whom Phoibos, or Sigurd, or Beo-
wulf, or Oidipous smite and slay. That the worship of the Serpent has nothing to do with these evil beasts is abundantly clear
from all the Phallic monuments of the East or West. In the
topes of Sanchi and Amravati the disks which represent the
Yoni predominate in every part of the design; the emblem is
worn with unmistakeable distinctness by every female figure,
carved within these disks, while above the multitude are seen, on
many of the disks, a group of women with their hands resting on
the linga, which they uphold. It may, indeed, be possible to
trace out the association which connects the Linga with the bull

in Sivaison, as denoting more particularly the male power, while the serpent in Jainaison and Vishnavism is found with the female emblem, the Yoni. So again in Egypt, some may discern in the bull Apis or Mnevis the predominance of the male idea in that country, while in Assyria or Palestine the Serpent or Agathos Daimon is connected with the altar of Baal.

CHAPTER III.

Mythology of the Ancients—Characteristics of the Pagan Deities—Doctrine of the Reciprocal Principles of Nature—Creation of the Egg—Creation and the Phallus—The Lotus—Osiris as the active, dispensing, and originating energy—Hesiod and the generative powers—Growth of Phallic Worship.

" **B**Y comparing all the varied legends of the East and West in conjunction," says a learned author, " we obtain the following outline of the mythology of the Ancients: It recognises, as the primary elements of things, two independent principles of the nature of Male and Female; and these, in mystic union, as the soul and body, constitute the Great Hermaphrodite Deity, THE ONE, the universe itself, consisting still of the two separate elements of its composition, modified though combined in one individual, of which all things are regarded but as parts. . . . . If we investigate the Pantheons of the ancient nations, we shall find that each, notwithstanding the variety of names, acknowledged the same deities and the same system of theology; and, however humble any of the deities may appear, each who has any claim to antiquity will be found ultimately, if not immediately, resolvable into one or other of the Primeval Principles, the Great God and Goddess of the Gentiles."[*]

"We must not be surprised," says Sir William Jones, "at finding, on a close examination, that the characters of all the Pagan deities, male and female, melt into each other, and at last into one or two, for it seems a well-founded opinion that the whole crowd of gods and goddesses in ancient Rome and modern Váránes mean only the Powers of Nature, and principally those of the Sun, expressed in a variety of ways and by a multitude of fanciful names."

* Cory's Ancient Fragments, Intro. 34.

The doctrine of the Reciprocal Principles of Nature, designated as active and passive, male and female, and often symbolized as the Sun and Moon, or the Sun and the Earth, was distinctly recognised in the mythological systems of America. It will be well to notice the *rationale* of this doctrine, and some of the more striking forms which, in the development of human ideas, it has assumed; for it may safely be claimed that under some of its aspects or modifications it has entered into every religious system, if, indeed, it has not been the nucleus of every mythology.

The idea of a creation, suggested by the existence of things, was, no doubt, the first result of human reasoning. The mode of the event, the manner in which it was brought about, was, it is equally unquestionable, the inquiry which next occupied the mind, and man deduced from the operations of nature around him his first theory of creation. From the egg, after incubation, he saw emerging the living bird, a phenomenon which, to his simple apprehension, was nothing less than an actual creation. How naturally then, how almost of necessity, did that phenomenon, one of the most obvious in nature, associate itself with his ideas of creation—a creation which he could not help recognising, but which he could not explain. The extent to which the egg, received as a symbol, entered into the early cosmogonies will appear in another and more appropriate connection.

By a similar process did the creative power come to be symbolized under the form of the Phallus, in it was recognised the cause of reproduction, or, as it appeared to the primitive man, of creation. So the Egyptians, in their refinement upon this idea, adopted the scarabæus as a symbol of the First Cause, the great hermaphrodite Unity, for the reason that they believed that insect to be both male and female, capable of self-inception and singular production, and possessed of the power of vitalizing its own worm.

It is well known that the Nymphœ, Lotus, or Water-Lily is held sacred throughout the East, and the various sects of that quarter of the globe represent their deities, either decorated with its flowers, holding it as a sceptre, or seated on a lotus throne or pedestal. "It is," says Maurice, "the sublime and hallowed symbol that perpetually occurs in oriental mythology, and not without substantial reason; for it is itself a lovely prodigy, and contains a treasure of physical instruction." The reason of its adoption as a symbol is explained by Mr. Payne Knight, and affords a beautiful illustration of the *rationale* of symbolism, and of the profound significance often hidden beneath apparently insignificant emblems. "This plant," observes Mr. Knight, "grows in the water, and amongst its broad leaves puts forth a flower, in the centre of which is formed its seed vessel, shaped like a bell or inverted cone, and punctured on the top with little cavities or cells, in which the seeds grow. The orifice of these cells being too small to let the seeds drop out when ripe, they shoot forth into new plants in the places where they are formed; the bulb of the vessel serving as a matrix to nourish them until large enough to burst it open and release themselves, after which, like other aquatic plants, they take root wherever the current deposits them. The plant, therefore, being thus productive of itself, and vegetating from its own matrix, without being fostered in the earth; was naturally adopted as a symbol of the productive power of waters upon which the active Spirit of the Creator acted in giving life and vegetation to matter. We accordingly find it employed in every part of the northern hemisphere where the symbolical religion, improperly called idolatry, existed."

Examples quoted illustrate the inductive powers by which un-aided reason arrives at its results, as well as the means by which it indicates them in the absence of a written language or of one capable of conveying abstract ideas. The mythological symbols of all early nations furnish ample evidence that it was thus they embodied or shadowed forth their conceptions—the germ of a symbolic system, which was afterwards extended to every manifestation of nature and every attribute of Divinity.

We may in this manner rationally and satisfactorily account for the origin of the doctrine of the reciprocal principles. Its universal acceptance establishes that it was deduced from the operations of that law so obviously governing all animated nature —that of reproduction or procreation.

In the Egyptian mythology, the Divine Osiris was venerated as the active, dispensing, or originating energy, and was symbolized as the Sun; Iris as terrene nature, the passive recipient, the producer; their annual offspring was Horus, the vernal season or infant year. The poet Hesiod, in the beginning of his Theogony, distinguishes the male and female, or generative and productive powers of Nature, as Ouranus and Gaia, Heaven and Earth. The celestial emblems of these powers were usually, as we have said, the Sun and Moon; the terrestrial, Fire and Earth. They were designed as Father and Mother; and their more obvious symbols, as has already been intimated, were the Phallus and Kteis, or the Lingam and Yoni of Hindustan.

That the worship of the phallus passed from India or from Ethiopia into Egypt, from Egypt into Asia Minor, and into Greece, is not so much a matter of astonishment—these nations communicated with each other; but that this worship existed in countries a long time unknown to the rest of the world—in many parts of America, with which the people of the Eastern Continent had formerly no communication — is an astonishing but well attested fact. When Mexico was discovered, there was found in the city of Panuco, the particular worship of the Phallus well established, its image was adorned in the temples; there were in the public places bas reliefs, which like those of India, represented in various manners the union of the two sexes. At Tlascalla, another city of Mexico, they revered the act of generation under the united symbols of the characteristic organs of the two sexes. Garcilasso de la Vega says—" that according to Blas Valera, the God of Luxury was called Tiazolteuli,'' but some writers say, " this is a mistake.'' One of the goddesses of the Mexican Pantheon was named Tiazolteotl, which Boturini describes as Venus unchaste, low, and abominable, the hieroglyphic of these men and women who are wholly abandoned, mingling promiscuously one with another, gratifying their bestial appetites like animals. Boturini is said to be not entirely correct in his apprehensions of the character of this goddess. She is Cinteotl, the goddess of Maize, under another aspect. Certain of the temples of India abound with sculptured representations of the symbols of Phallic Worship, and if we turn to the temples of Central America, which in many respects exhibit a strict correspondence with those of India, we find precisely the same symbols, separate and in combination.

CHAPTER IV.

Ancient Monuments of the West—The Valley of the Mississippi—
Numerous Earthworks of the Western States—Theory as to origin
of the mounds—The "Defence" Theory—The Religious Theory
—Earthwork of the "Great Serpent" on Bush Creek—The
"Alligator," Ohio—The "Cross," Pickaway County—Structures
of Wisconsin—Mr. Pigeon's Drawings—Significance of the Earth-
mounds—The Egg and Man's Primitive Ideas—The Egg as a
Symbol—Birth of Brahma—Aristophanes and his "Comedy of
the Birds"—The Hymn to Protogones—The Chinese and Creation
—The Mundane or Orphic Egg—Kneph—Mr. Gliddon's replies
to certain enquiries—The Orphic Theogony and the Egg—The
Great Unity.

THE ancient monuments of the Western United States
consist for the most part of elevations and embankments
of earth and stone, erected with great labour and manifest design.
In connection with these, more or less intimate, are found
various minor relics of art, consisting of ornaments and imple-
ments of many kinds, some of them composed of metal but most
of stone.

These remains are spread over a vast amount of country.
They are found on the sources of the Alleghany, in the western
part of the state of New York on the east; and extend thence
westwardly along the southern shore of Lake Erie, and through
Michigan and Wisconsin, to Iowa and the Nebraska territory
on the west. Some ancient works, probably belonging to the
same system with those of the Mississippi valley and erected by
the same people, occur upon the Susquehanna river as far down
as the Valley of Wyoming in Pennsylvania. The mound builders
seem to have skirted the southern border of Lake Erie, and
spread themselves in diminished numbers over the western part
of the State of New York, along the shores of Lake Ontario to

the St. Lawrence river. They penetrated into the interior, eastward, as far as the county of Onondaga, where some slight
vestiges of their work still exist. These seem to have been their
limits at the north-east. We have no record of their occurrence
above the great lakes. Carner mentions some on the shores of
Lake Pepin, and some are said to occur near Lake Travers, under
the 46th parallel of latitude. Lewis and Clarke saw them on
the Missouri river, one thousand miles above its junction with
the Mississippi; and they have been observed on the Kanzas and
Platte and on other remote western rivers. They are found all
over the intermediate country, and spread over the valley of the
Mississippi to the Gulf of Mexico. They line the shores of the
Gulf from Texas to Florida, and extend in diminished numbers
into South Carolina. They occur in great numbers in Ohio,
Indiana, Illinois, Wisconsin, Missouri, Arkansas, Kentucky,
Tennessee, Louisiana, Mississippi, Alabama, Georgia, Florida
and Texas. They are found in less numbers in the Western
portions of New York, Pennsylvania, Virginia, and North and
South Carolina; as also in Michigan, Iowa, and in the Mexican
territory beyond the Rio Grande del Norte. In short, they
occupy the entire basin of the Mississippi and its tributaries, as
also the fertile plains along the Gulf.

Although possessing throughout certain general points of
resemblance going to establish a kindred origin, these works,
nevertheless, resolve themselves into three grand geographical
divisions, which present in many respects striking contrasts, yet
so gradually merge into each other that it is impossible to determine where one series terminates and the other begins. In the
region bordering upon the upper lakes, to a certain extent in
Michigan, Iowa and Missouri, but particularly in Wisconsin, we
find a succession of remains, entirely singular in their form and
presenting but slight analogy to any others of which we have in

any portion of the globe. The larger proportion of these are structures of earth bearing the forms of beasts, birds, reptiles, and even of men; they are frequently of gigantic dimensions, constituting huge *basso-relievos* upon the face of the country. They are very numerous and in most cases occur in long and apparently dependent ranges. In connection with them are found many conical mounds and occasional short lines of embankment, in rare instances forming enclosures. These animal effigies are mainly confined to Wisconsin, and extend across that territory from Ford du Lac in a south-western direction, ascending the Fox river and following the general course of Rock and Wisconsin rivers to the Mississippi. They may be much more extensively disseminated; but it is here only that they have been observed in considerable numbers. In Michigan, as also in Iowa and Missouri, similar elevations of more or less outline are said to occur. They are represented as dispersed in ranges like the buildings of a modern city, and covering sometimes an arc of many acres.

The number of these ancient remains is well calculated to excite surprise, and has been adduced in support of the hypothesis that they are most if not all of them natural formations, "the result of diluvial action," modified perhaps in some instances, but never erected by man. Of course no such suggestion was ever made by individuals who had enjoyed the opportunity of seeing and investigating them. Simple structures of earth could not possibly bear more palpable evidences of an artificial origin than do most of the western monuments. The evidences in support of this assertion, derived from the form, structure, position and contents of these remains, sufficiently appear in the pages of this work.

The structure, not less than the form and position of a large number of the Earthworks of the West, and especially of the

Scioto valley, render it clear that they were erected for other than
defensive purposes. The small dimensions of most of the circles,
the occurrence of the ditch interior to the embankments, and the
fact that many of them are completely commanded by adjacent
heights, are some of the circumstances which may be mentioned
as sustaining this conclusion. We must seek, therefore, in the
connection in which these works are found and in the character
of the mounds, if such there be within their walls, for the secret
of their origin.   And it may be observed that it is here we
discover evidences still more satisfactory and conclusive than are
furnished by their small dimensions and other circumstances
above mentioned, that they were not intended for defence. Thus,
when we find an enclosure containing a number of mounds, all
of which it is capable of demonstration were religious in their
purposes or in some way connected with the superstitions of the
people who built them, the conclusion is irresistible that the
enclosure itself was also deemed sacred and thus set apart as
" tabooed '' or consecrated ground—especially where it is obvious
at the first glance that it possesses none of the requisites of a
military work.   But it is not to be concluded that those
enclosures alone, which contain mounds of the description here
named, were designed for sacred purposes. We have reason to
believe that the religious system of the mound builders, like that
of the Aztecs, exercised among them a great if not controlling
influence. Their government may have been, for aught we know,
a government of priesthood ; one in which the priestly and civil
functions were jointly exercised, and one sufficiently powerful to
have secured in the Mississippi valley, as it did in Mexico, the
erection of many of those vast monuments which for ages will
continue to challenge the wonder of men.   There may have been
certain superstitious ceremonies, having no connection with the
purposes of the mounds, carried on in the enclosures specially

dedicated to them.   It is a conclusion which every day's investi-
gation and observation has tended to confirm, that most, perhaps
all, of the earthworks not manifestly defensive in their character
were in some way connected with the superstitious rights of the
builders, though in what manner, it is, and perhaps ever will be,
impossible satisfactorily to determine.

By far the most extraordinary and interesting earthwork
discovered in the West is the great Serpent, situate on Brush
Creek at a point known as the " Three Forks," near the north
line of Adams county, Ohio.   It occupies the summit of a high
crescent-form hill or spur of land, rising a hundred and fifty feet
above the level of Brush Creek, which washes its base.   The
side of the hill next the stream presents a perpendicular wall of
rock, while the other slopes rapidly, though it is not so steep as
to preclude cultivation.   The top of the hill is not level but
slightly convex, and presents a very even surface one hundred
and fifty feet wide by one thousand long, measuring from its
extremity to the point where it connects with the table land.
Conforming to the curve of the hill and occupying its very
summit is the serpent, its head resting near the point and its
body winding back for seven hundred feet in graceful undulations,
terminating in a triple coil at the tail.   The entire length, if
extended, would be not less than one thousand feet.   The neck
of the serpent is stretched out and slightly curved, and its mouth
is opened wide as if in the act of swallowing or ejecting an oval
figure which rests partially within the distended jaws.   This oval
is formed by an embankment of earth, without any perceptible
opening, four feet in height, and is perfectly regular in outline,
its transverse and conjugate diameters being one hundred and
sixty and eighty feet respectively.   The ground within the oval
is slightly elevated; a small circular elevation of large stones
much burned once existed in its centre, but they have been

thrown down and scattered by some ignorant visitor, under the
prevailing impression probably that gold was hidden beneath
them.   The point of the hill within which this egg-shaped figure
rests seems to have been artificially cut to conform to its outline,
leaving a smooth platform, ten feet wide and somewhat inclin-
ing inwards, all around it.

Upon either side of the serpent's head extend two small
triangular elevations ten or twelve feet over.   They are not high,
and although too distinct to be overlooked, are yet much too
much obliterated to be satisfactorily traced.

An effigy in the form of an alligator occurs near Granville,
Licking county, Ohio, upon a high hill or headland; in connection with which there are unmistakeable evidences of an altar,
similar to that in conjunction with the work just named.   It is
known in the vicinity as " the Alligator," which designation has
been adopted for want of a better, although the figure bears as
close a resemblance to the lizard as any other reptile.   It is
placed transversely to the point of land on which it occurs, the
head pointing to the south-west.   The total length from the
point of the nose following the curve of the tail to the tip is
about two hundred and fifty feet, the breadth of the body forty
feet, and the length of the feet or paws each thirty-six feet.   The
ends of the paws are a little broader than the remaining portions
of the same, as if the spread of the toes had been originally
indicated.   Some parts of the body are more elevated than others,
an attempt having evidently been made to preserve the proportions of the object copied.   The outline of the figure is clearly
defined; its average height is not less than four feet; at the
shoulders it is six feet in altitude.   Upon the inner side of the
effigy is an elevated circular space covered with stones which
have been burned.   This has been denominated an altar.

It seems more than probable that this singular effigy, like that last described, had its origin in the superstition of its makers. It was perhaps the high place where sacrifices were made on stated or extraordinary occasions, and where the ancient people gathered to celebrate the rites of their unknown worship. Its position and all the circumstances attending it certainly favour such a conclusion.

The same is true of a work in the form of a cross, occupying a like situation near the village of Tarlton, Pickaway County, Ohio. From these premises, we are certainly justified in concluding that these several effigies had probably a cognate design, possessed a symbolical significance, and were conspicuous objects of religious regard, and that on certain occasions sacrifices were made on the altars within or near them.

The only structures sustaining any analogy to these are found in Wisconsin and the extreme North-West. There we find great numbers of mounds bearing the forms of animals of various kinds, and entering into a great variety of combinations with each other, and with conical mounds and lines of embankments, which are also abundant. They are usually found on the low, level, or un-dulating prairies, and seldom in such conspicuous positions as those discovered in Ohio. Whether they were built by the same people with the latter, and had a common design and purpose, it is not undertaken to say, nor is it a question into which we pro-pose to enter.

It is an interesting fact that amongst the animal effigies of Wisconsin, structures in the form of serpents are of frequent occurrence.

Some years ago, Mr. Pigeon, of Virginia, made drawings of a number of these, and he stated that near the junction of the St. Peter's with the Mississippi River were a large number of mounds and monuments, consisting—1st, of a circle and square in combination, as at Circleville, in Ohio, the sole difference being a large truncated mound in the centre of the square, as well as in the centre of the circle, with a platform round its base; 2nd, near by, the effigy of a gigantic animal resembling the elk, in length one hundred and ninety-five feet; 3rd, in the same vicinity, a large conical mound, three hundred feet in diameter at the base, and thirty feet in height, its summit covered with charcoal. This mound was surrounded by one hundred and twenty smaller mounds, disposed in the form of a circle. Twelve miles to the westward of these, and within sight of them, was a large conical truncated mound, sixty feet in diameter at the bottom, and eighteen feet high, built upon a raised platform or bottom. It was surrounded by a circle three hundred and sixty-five feet in circumference. Entwined around this circle, in a triple coil, was an embankment, in the form of a serpent, two thousand three hundred and ten feet in length. This embankment, at the centre of the body, was eighteen feet in diameter, but diminished towards the head and tail in just proportion. The elevation of the head was four feet, of the body six feet, of the tail two feet. The central mound was capped with blue clay, beneath which was sand mixed with charcoal and ashes.

Mounds arranged in serpentine form have also been found in Iowa, at a place formerly known as Prairie La Porte, afterwards called Gottenburgh. Also at a place seven miles north of these on Turkey River, where the range was two and a half miles long, the mounds occurring at regular intervals. Twenty miles to the westward of this locality was the effigy of a great serpent with that of a tortoise in front of its mouth. This structure was found to be one thousand and four feet long, eighteen feet broad at its widest part, and six feet high; the tortoise was eighteen by twelve feet.

Mr. Pigeon gave accounts of many other structures, tending to illustrate and confirm the opinions advanced respecting the religious and symbolical character and design of many, if not all, the more regular earth-works of the Western States. Thirty miles west of Prairie Du Chien, he found a circle enclosing a pentagon, which in its turn enclosed another circle, within which was a conical truncated mound. The outer circle was twelve hundred feet in circumference, the embankment twelve feet broad and from three to five feet high. The entrance was on the east. The mound was thirty-six feet in diameter by twelve feet high. Its summit was composed of white pipe-clay, beneath which was found a large quantity of mica in sheets. It exhibited abundant traces of fire.

Four miles distant from this, on the lowlands of the Kickapoo River, Mr. Pigeon discovered a mound with eight radiating points, undoubtedly designed to represent the Sun. It was sixty feet in diameter at the base, and three feet high. The points extended outwards about nine feet. Surrounding this mound were five crescent-shaped mounds so arranged as to constitute a circle. Many analogous structures were discovered at other places, both in Wisconsin and Iowa. At Cappile Bluffs, on the Mississippi River, was found a conical, truncated mound, surrounded by nine radiating effigies of men, the heads pointing inwards.

Probably no one will hesitate in ascribing to work just described, some extraordinary significance. It cannot be supposed to be the offspring of an idle fancy or a savage whim. It bears, in its position and the harmony of its structure, the evidences of design, and it seems to have been begun and finished in accordance with a matured plan, and not to have been the result of successive and unmeaning combinations. It is probably not a work for defence, for there is nothing to defend; on the contrary,

it is clearly and unmistakably, in form and attitude, the representation of a serpent, with jaws distended, in the act of swallowing or ejecting an oval figure, which may be distinguished, from
the suggestions of analogy, as an egg. Assuming for the entire
structure a religious origin, it can be regarded only as the recognised symbol of some grand mythological idea. What abstract
conception was thus embodied ; or what vast event thus typically
commemorated, we have no certain means of knowing! Analogy,
however, although too often consulted on trivial grounds, fur-
nishes us with gleams of light, of greater or less steadiness, as
our appeals to its assistance happen to be conducted, on every
subject connected with man's beliefs. We proceed now to discover what light reason and analogy shed upon the singular structure before us.

Naturally, and almost of necessity, the egg became associated
with man's primitive idea of a creation. It aptly symbolised that
primordial, quiescent state of things which preceded their vitali-
zation and activity—the inanimate chaos, before life began, when
" the earth was without form and void, and darkness was upon
the face of the deep."   It was thus received in the early cosmogonies, in all of which the vivification of the Mundane Egg
constituted the act of creation ; from it sprang the world resplen-
dent in glory and teeming with life.

Faber says—" The ancient pagans, in almost every part of
the globe, were wont to symbolize the world by an Egg. Hence
this symbol is introduced into the cosmogonies of nearly all
nations, and there are few persons even among those who have not
made mythology their study, to whom the Mundane Egg is not
perfectly familiar. It was employed, not only to represent the
earth, but also the Universe in its largest extent."*

" The world," says Menu, " was all darkness, undiscernible,
undistinguishable, altogether in a profound sleep, till the Self-

* Origin Pagan Idol., Vol. 1, p. 175.

Existent, Invisible God (Brahm), making it manifest with five elements and other glorious forms, perfectly dispelled the gloom. Desiring to raise up creatures by an emanation from his own essence, he first created the waters, and inspired them with power of motion; by that power was produced a golden egg, blazing like a thousand stars, in which was born Brahma, the great parent of national beings, that which is the invisible cause, self-existent, but unperceived. This divinity having dwelt in the Egg through revolving years, himself meditating upon himself, divided into two equal parts, and from these halves he framed the heavens and the earth, placing in the midst the subtil ether, the eight points of the world, and the permanent receptacle of the waters.''

The above is Maurice's translation. Sir William Jones renders it:—" The sole, self-existent power, having willed to produce various beings from his own divine substance, first, with a thought created the waters, and placed in them a productive seed. That seed became an egg, bright as gold, blazing like the luminary with a thousand beams, and in that egg was born himself, in the form of Brahma, the great forefather of all spirits.''

Aristophanes, in his Comedy of the Birds, is thought to have given the notions of cosmogony, ancient even in his days. " Chaos, Night, black Erebus, and wide Tartarus first existed: there was neither earth, nor air, nor heaven; but in the bosom of Erebus black-winged Night produced an Aerial Egg, from which was born golden-pinioned Love (Phanes), and he, the Great Universal Father, begot our race out of dark Chaos, in the midst of wide-spreading Tartarus, and called us into light.''

We find this conception clearly embodied in one of the Orphic fragments, the Hymn to Protogones, who is equivalent to Phanes, the Life-giver, Priapus, or Generator.

" I invoke thee, oh Protogones, two-fold, great, wandering through
     the ether ;
Egg-Born rejoicing in thy golden wings ;
Bull-faced, the Generator of the blessed and of mortal men ;
The much-renowned Light, the far celebrated Ericapæus ;
Ineffable, occult, impetuous all-glittering strength ;
Who scatterest the twilight cloud of darkness from the eyes,
And roam'st through the world upon the flight of thy wings,
Bringing forth the brilliant and all-pure light ; wherefore I invoke
     thee, as Phanes,
As Priapus the King, and as the dark-faced splendour,—
Come, thou blessed being, full of Metis (wisdom) and generation,
     come in joy
To thy sacred, ever-varying mysteries."

We have, according to these early notions, the egg representing Being simply ; Chaos, the great void from which, by the will
of the superlative Unity, proceeds the generative or creative influence, designated among the Greeks as " Phanes," " Golden-
pinioned Love," " The Universal Father," " Egg-born Protogones " (the latter Zeus or Jupiter) ; in India as " Brahma," the
" Great Parent of Rational Creatures," the " Father of the
Universe;" and in Egypt as " Ptha," the " Universal Creator."

The Chinese, whose religious conceptions correspond generally
with those of India, entertained similar notions of the origin of
things. They set forth that Chaos, before the creation, existed
in the form of a vast egg, in which was contained the principles
of all things. Its vivification, among them also, constituted the
act of creation.

According to this and other authorities, the vivification of the
Mundane Egg is allegorically represented in the temple of
Daibod, in Japan, by a nest egg, which is shown floating in an
expanse of waters against which a bulb (everywhere an emblem
of generative energy, and prolific heat, the Sun) is striking with
his horns.

" Near Lemisso, in the Island of Cyprus, is still to be seen a gigantic egg-shaped vase, which 'is supposed to represent the Mundane or Orphic Egg. It is of stone, and measures thirty feet in circumference. Upon one side, in a semi-circular niche, is sculptured a bull, the emblem of productive energy. This figure is understood to signify the Tauric constellation, "The Stars of Abundance," with the heliacal or cosmical rising of which was connected the return of the mystic reinvigorating principle of animal fecundity." *

In the opinions above mentioned, many other nations of the ancient world, the Egyptians, the Assyrians, the Phœnicians, and the Indo-Scythiac nations of Europe participated. They not only supported the propriety of the allegory, says Maurice, from the perfection of its external form, but fancifully extended the allusion to its interior composition, comparing the pure white shell to the fair expanse of heaven; the fluid, transparent white, to the cir- cumambient air, and the more solid yolk to the central earth.

Even the Polynesians entertained the same general notions. The tradition of the Sandwich Islanders is that a bird (with them it is an emblem of Deity) laid an egg upon the waters which burst of itself and produced the Islands.

The great hermaphrodite first principle in its character of Unity, the Supreme Monad, the highest conception of Divinity was denominated Kneph or Cnuphis among the Egyptian. According to Plutarch this god was without beginning and with- out end, the One, uncreated and eternal, above all, and compre- hending all. And as Brahm, "the Self-existent Incorruptible ". Unity of the Hindus, by direction of His energetic will upon the expanse of chaos, "with a thought " (say Menu) produced a "golden egg blazing like a thousand stars," from which sprung Brahma, the Creator; so according to the mystagogues, Kneph

* Landseer's Sabæan Res.

the Unity of Egypt, was represented as a serpent thrusting from his mouth an egg, from which proceeds the divinity *Phtha*, the active creative power, equivalent in all his attributes to the Indian Brahma.

That Kneph was symbolized by the ancient Egyptians under the form of serpent is well known. It is not, however, so well established that the act of creation was allegorically represented in Egypt by the symbolic serpent thrusting from its mouth an egg, although no doubt of the fact seems to have been entertained by the various authors who have hitherto written on the Cosmogony and Mythology of the primitive nations of the East. With the view of ascertaining what new light has been thrown upon the subject by the investigations of the indefatigable Champollion and his followers — whose researches among the monuments and records of Ancient Egypt have been attended with most remarkable results — the following inquiries were addressed to Mr. G. R. Gliddon (U.S. Consul at Cairo), a gentleman distinguished for his acquaintance with Egyptian science, and his zeal in disseminating information on a subject too little understood:—

" Do the serpent and the egg, separate or in combination, occur among the Egyptian symbols and if they occur what significance seem to have been assigned them? Was the serpent in any way associated with the worship of the sun or the kindred worship of the Phallus? "

To these inquiries Mr. Gliddon replied as follows:—" In respect to your first inquiry; I concede at once that the general view of the Greco-Roman antiquity, the oriental traditions collected, often indiscriminately, by the Fathers and the concurring suffrages of all occidental Mythologists, attribute the compound symbol of the Serpent combined with the Mundane Egg to the Egyptians. Modern criticism however, coupled with

the application of the tests furnished by Champollion le-Jeune
and his followers since 1827 to the hieroglyphics of Egypt, has
recognised so many exotic fables and so much real ignorance of
Egyptology in the accounts concerning that mystified country,
handed down to us from the schools of Alexandria and Byzantium, that at the present hour science treads doubtingly, where
but a few years ago it was fashionable to make the most sweep-
ing assertions; and we now hesitate before qualifying, as
Egyptian in origin, ideas that belong to the Mythologies of other
eastern nations. Classical authority, correct enough when treating on the philosophy and speculative theories of Ptolemaic and
Roman Alexandria, is generally at fault when in respect to
questions belonging to anterior or Pharaonic times. Whatever
we derive through the medium of the Alexandrines, and
especially through their successors, the Gnostics, must by the
Archæologist be received with suspicion.

After this you will not be surprised if I express doubts as to
existence of the myth of the Serpent and Egg in the Cosmogony
of the early Egyptians. It is lamentably true that, owing to
twenty centuries of destruction, so fearfully wrought out by
Mohammed Ali, we do not up to this day possess one tithe of the
monuments or papyri bequeathed to posterity by the recording
genius of the Khime. It is possible that this myth may have
been contained in the vast amount of hieroglyphical literature
now lost to us. But the fact that in no instance whatever, amid
the myriads of inscribed or sculptured documents extant, does the
symbol of the Serpent and the Egg occur, militates against the
assumption of this, perhaps Phœnician myth, as originally
Egyptian. "The worship of the Serpent," observes Ampère,
"by the Ophites may certainly have a real connection with the
choice of the Egyptian symbol by which Divinity is designated
in the paintings and hieroglyphics, and which is the Serpent

Uræus (Basilisk royal, of the Greeks) the seraph set up by
Moses.   Se Ra Ph is the singular of seraphim, meaning Semiticé,
splendour, fire, light; emblematic of the fiery disk of the sun
and which, under the name of Nehushtan—" Serpent Dragon "—
was broken up by the reforming Hezekiah (2 Kings, 18, 4); or
with the serpent with wings and feet, which we see represented
in the Funeral Rituals; but the serpent is everywhere in the
Mythologies and Cosmogonies of the East, and we cannot be
assured that the serpent of the Ophites (any more than that
emitting or encircling the Mundane Egg) was Egyptian rather
than Jewish, Persian, or Hindustanee."

" No serpents found in the hieroglyphics bear, so far as I can
perceive, any direct relation to the Ouine Myth, nor have Egyptian Eggs any direct connection with the Cosmogonical Serpent.
The egg, under certain conditions, seems to denote the idea of a
human body.   It is also used as a phonetic sign S, and when
combined with T, is the determinative of the feminine gender;
in which sense exclusively it is sometimes placed close to a
serpent in hieroglyphical legends."

" My doubts apply in attempting to give a specific answer to
your specific question; i.e., the direct connection, in Egyptian
Mythology, of the Serpent and the Cosmogonical Egg.   In the
" Book of the Dead," according to a MS. translation favoured
me by the erudite Egyptologist, Mr. Birch, of the British
Museum, allusion is made to the " great mundane egg " addressed
by the deceased, which seems to refer to the winds or the atmos-
phere—again the deceased exclaims ' I have raised myself up in
the form of the great Hawk which comes out of the Egg (i.e.,
the Sun).'

" I do not here perceive any immediate allusion to the duplex
emblem of the egg combined with the serpent, the subject of
your query.

"Yet a reservation must be made in behalf of your very consistent hypothesis — supported, as I allow, by all oriental and classical authority, if not possibly by the Egyptian documents yet undeciphered—which hypothesis is Euclidean. 'Things which are equal to the same are equal to one another.' Now if the 'Mundane Egg' be in the papyric rituals the equivalent to Sun, and that by other hieroglyphical texts we prove the Sun to be, in Egypt as elsewhere, symbolized by the figure of a Serpent, does not the 'ultima ratio' resolve both emblems into one? Your grasp of this Old and New World Question renders it superfluous that I should now posite the syllogism. I content myself by referring you to the best of authorities. One point alone is what I would venture to suggest to your philosophical acumen, in respect to ancient 'parallelisms' between the metaphysical conceptions of radically distinct nations (if you please, 'species' of mankind, at geographically different centres of *origins*, compelled of necessity in ages anterior to alphabetical record to express their ideas by pictures, figurative or symbolical). It is that man's mind has always conceived, everywhere in the same method, everything that relates to him; because the inability in which his intelligence is circumscribed, to figure to his mind's eye existence distinct from his own, constrains him to devolve in the pictorial or sculptural delineation of his thoughts, within the same circle of ideas; and, ergo, the figurative representative of his ideas must ever be, in all ages and countries, the reflex of the same hypotheses, material or physical. May not the emblem of the Serpent and Egg, as well in the New as in the Old World, have originated from a similar organic law without thereby establishing intercourse? Is not your serpent a "rattle snake" and, ergo, purely American? Are not Egyptian Serpents all purely Nilotic? The metaphysical idea of the Cosmogonical Serpent may be one and the same; but does not the zoological diversity of representation prove that America, three thousand years ago, could have no possible intercourse with Egypt, Phœnicia, or *vice versa*?

" Such being the only values attach$\ni$d to Serpents and eggs in Egyptian hieroglyphics it is arduous to speculate whether an esoteric significance did or did not exist between those emblems in the, to us, unknown Cosmogony of the Theban and Memphite Colleges. I, too, could derive inferences and deduce analogies between the attributes of the God Knuphis, or the God Ptha, and the ' Mundane Egg ' recorded by Eusebius, Jamblichus, and a wilderness of classical authorities, but I fear with no very satisfactory result. It is, however, due to Mr. Bonomi, to cite his language on this subject. Speaking of the colossal state of Rameses Sesostris at Metraheni, in a paper read before the Royal Society of Literature, London, June, 1845, he observes, ' There is one more consideration connected with the hiero-glyphics of the great oval of the belt, though not affecting the preceding argument; it is the oval or egg which occurs between the figure of Ptha and the staff of which the usual signification is Son or Child, but which by a kind of two-fold meaning, common in the details of sculpture of this period (the 18th or 19th Dynasty, say B.C. 1500 or 1200), I am inclined to believe refers also to the myth or doctrine preserved in the writings of the Greek authors, as belonging to Vulcan and said to be derived from Egypt, viz., the doctrine of the Mundane Egg. Now, although in no Egyptian sculpture of the remote period of this statue has there been found any allusion to this doctrine, it is most distinctly hinted at in one of the age of the Ptolomies; and I am inclined to think it was imported from the East by Sesostris, where, in confirmation of its existence at a very remote period, I would quote the existence of those egg-shaped basaltic stones, embossed with various devices and covered with cuneatic inscriptions, which are brought from some of the ancient cities of Mesopotamia.

' In respect to your final inquiry, I may observe that I can
luce nothing from the hieroglyphics to connect, directly,
llic Worship with the solar emblem of the Serpent. In
itic tongues, the same root signifies Serpent and Phallus ;
in different senses are solar emblems.''

In the Orphic Theogony a similar origin is ascribed to the
from which springs " the Egg-born Protogones,'' the Greek
iterpart of the Egyptian Phtha. The egg in this instance
proceeds from the pre-eminent Unity, the Serpent God, the
comparable Cronus,'' or Hercules. (Bryant, quoting Athena-
s, observes — " Hercules was esteemed the chief god, the
e as Cronus, and was said to have produced the Mundane
. He is represented in the Orphic Theology, under the
d symbol of a lion and a serpent, and sometimes of a serpent
.'')

Cronus was originally esteemed the Supreme, as is manifest
his being called Il or Ilus, which is the same with the
rew El and, according to St. Jerome, one of the ten names of
. Damascius, in the life of Isidorus, mentions distinctly
Cronus was worshipped under the name of El, who, accord-
to Sanchoniathon, had no one superior or antecedent to
self.

Brahm, Cronus, and Kneph each represented the mystical
n of the reciprocal or active and passive principles. Most,
t all, the primitive nations recognised this Supreme Unity,
ough they did not all assign him a name. He was the
tor of Gods, who were the Demiurgs of the Universe, the
tors of all rational beings, angels and men, and the architects
e world.

The early writers exhaust language in endeavous to express
lofty character and attributes, and the superlative power and
ity of this great Unity, the highest conception of which man

is capable.　He is spoken of in the sacred book of the Hindus as the "Almighty, infinite, eternal, incomprehensible, self-existent Being; he who sees everything, though never seen; he who is not to be compassed by description; he from whom the universe proceeds; who reigns supreme, the light of all lights; whose power is too infinite to be imagined; is Brahm, the One Being, True and Unknown." *

The supreme God of Gods of the Hindus was less frequently expressed by the name Brahm than by the mystical syllable O'M, which corresponded to the Hebrew Jehovah.　Strange as the remark may seem to most minds, it is nevertheless true, that the fundamental principles of the Hindu religion were those of pure Monotheism, the worship of one supreme and only God. Brahm was regarded as too mighty to be named; and, while his symbolized or personified attributes were adored in gorgeous temples, not one was erected to him.　The holiest verse of the Vedas is paraphrased as follows:

"Perfect truth; perfect happiness; without equal; immortal; absolute unity; whom neither speech can describe nor mind comprehend; all-pervading; all-transcending; delighted by his own boundless intelligence, not limited by space or time; without feet, moving swiftly; without hands, grasping all worlds; without ears, all-hearing, understanding all; without cause, the first of all causes; all-ruling; all-powerful; the Creator, Preserver, and Transformer of all things; such is the Great One, Brahm."

The character and power of Kneph are indicated in terms no less lofty and comprehensive than those applied to the omnipotent Brahm.　He is described in the ancient Hermetic books as the "first God, immovable in the solitude of his Unity, the fountain of all things, the root of all primary, intelligible, existing forms, the God of Gods, before the etherial and empyrean Gods and the celestial."

* Coleman's Hind. Mythology.

In America this great Unity, this God of Gods, was equally recognised.   In Mexico as Teotl, "he who is all in himself" (Tloque Nahuaque); in Peru as Varicocha, the "Soul of the Universe;" in Central America and Yucatan as Stunah Ku or Hunab Ku, "God of Gods, the incorporeal origin of all things." And as the Supreme Brahm of the Hindus, "whose name was unutterable," was worshipped under no external form and had neither temples nor altars erected to him, so the Supreme Teot! and the corresponding Varicocha and Hunab Ku," whose names,'' says the Spanish conquerors, "were spoken only with extreme dread,`` were without an image or an outward form of worship for the reason, according to the same authorities, that each was regarded as the Invisible and Unknown God.

The Mundane Egg, received as a symbol of original, passive, unorganized, formless nature, became associated, in conformity with primitive notions, with other symbols referring to the creative force or vitalizing influence.   Thus in the Hindu cosmogony Brahma is represented, after long inertia, as arranging the passive elements, "creating the world and all visible things." Under the form of the emblematic bull the generative energy was represented breaking the quiescent egg.   Encircled by the folds of the agatho-demon, a type of the active principle, it was suspended aloft at the temples of Tyre.   For the serpent, like the bull, was an emblem of the sun or of the attributes of that luminary—itself the celestial emblem of the "Universal Father," the procreative power of nature.   "Everywhere," says Faber, "we find the great father exhibiting himself in the form of a serpent, and everywhere we find the serpent invested with the attributes of the Great Father and partaking of the honours which were paid him." *

Under this view, therefore, we may regard the compound symbol of the serpent and the egg, though specifically allusive to

* Origin Pagan Idol., vol. 1, p. 45.

the general creation, as an illustration of the doctrine of the reciprocal principles which, as we have already seen, enters largely into the entire fabric of primitive philosophy and mythology.

Thus have we shewn that the grand conception of a Supreme Unity and the doctrine of the reciprocal principles existed in America in a well defined and easily recognised form.

Our present inquiry relates to the symbols by which they were represented in both continents. That these were not usually arbitrary, but resulted from associations, generally of an obvious kind, will be readily admitted.

CHAPTER V.

The Sun and Fire as emblems—The Serpent and the Sun—Taut and the Serpent—Horapollo and the Serpent symbol—Sanchoniathon and the Serpent—Ancient Mysteries of Osiris, &c.—Rationale of the connection of Solar, Phallic, and Serpent Worship—The Aztec Pantheon—Mexican Gods—The Snake in Mexican Mythology—The Great Father and Mother—Quetzalcoatl, the Feathered Serpent— Researches of Stephens and Catherwood—Discoveries of Mr. Stephens.

THAT fire should be taken to be the physical, of what the sun is the celestial emblem; is sufficiently apparent; we can readily understand also how the bull, the goat, or ram, the phallus, and other symbols should have the same import; also how naturally and almost inevitably and universally the sun came to symbolize the active principle, the vivifying power, and how obviously the egg symbolized the passive elements of nature, but how the serpent came to possess, as a symbol, a like significance with these is not so obvious. That it did so, however, cannot be doubted, and the proofs will appear as we proceed; likewise that it sometimes symbolized the great hermaphrodite first principle, the Supreme Unity of the Greeks and Egyptians.

Although generally, it did not always symbolize the sun, or the power of which the sun is an emblem; but, invested with various meanings, it entered widely into the primitive mythologies. It typified wisdom, power, duration, the good and evil principles, life, reproduction — in short, in Egypt, Syria, Greece, India, China, Scandinavia, America, everywhere in the globe it has been a prominent emblem. In the somewhat poetical language of a learned author, " It entered into the mythology of every nation, consecrated almost every temple, symbolized almost every deity, was imagined in the heavens, stamped on the earth, and

E

ruled in the realms of everlasting sorrow.'' Its general acceptance seems to have been remarked at a very early period. It
arrested the attention of the ancient sages, who assigned a variety
of reasons for its adoption, founded upon the natural history of
the reptile. Among these speculations, none are more curious
than those preserved by Sanchoniathon, who says:—" Taut first
attributed something of the Divine nature to the Serpent, in
which he was followed by the Phœnicians and Egyptians. For
this animal was esteemed by him to be the most inspirited of all
reptiles, and of a fiery nature, inasmuch as it exhibits an in-
credible celerity, moving by its spirit, without hands or feet, or
any of the external members by which the other animals effect
their motion; and, in its progress, it assumes a variety of forms,
moving in a spiral course, and darting forward with whatever
degree of swiftness it pleases.''

It is, moreover, long lived, and has the quality not only of
putting off its old age, and assuming a second youth, but of re-
ceiving at the same time an augmentation of its size and strength;
and when it has filled the appointed measure of its existence, it
consumes itself, as Taut has laid down in the Sacred Books, upon
which account this animal is received into the sacred rites and
mysteries.

Horapollo, referring to the serpent symbol, says of it:—
" When the Egyptians would represent the Universe they de-
lineate a serpent bespeckled with variegated scales, devouring its
own tail, the scales intimating the stars in the Universe. The
animal is extremely heavy, as is the earth, and extremely slippery
like the water, moreover, it every year puts off its old age with its
skin, as in the Universe the annual period effects a corresponding
change and becomes renovated, and the making use of its own
body for food implies that all things whatever, which are generated by divine providence in the world, undergo a corruption
into them again.''

Nothing is more certain than that the serpent at a very remote period was regarded with high veneration as the most mysterious of living creatures. Its habits were imperfectly understood, and it was invested, as we perceive from the above quotations, with the most extraordinary qualities. Alike the object of fear, admiration, and wonder, it is not surprising that it became early connected with man's superstitions but how it obtained so general a predominance it is difficult to understand.

Perhaps there is no circumstance in the natural history of the serpent more striking than that alluded to by Sanchoniathon, viz.: the annual sloughing of its skin, or supposed rejuvenation.

> "As an old serpent casts his sealy vest,
> Wreaths in the Sun, in youthful glory dressed,
> So when Alcides' mortal mould resign'd,
> His better part enlarged, and grew refin'd."—OVID.

It was probably this which connected it with the idea of an eternal succession of forms, constant reproduction and dissolution, a process which was supposed by the ancients to have been for ever going on in nature. This doctrine is illustrated in the notion of a succession of Ages which prevailed among the Greeks, corresponding to the Yugs of the Hindus, and Suns of the aboriginal Mexicans. It is further illustrated by the annual dissolution and renovation exhibited in the succession of the seasons, and which was supposed to result from the augmentation and decline of the active principle, the Sun.

The mysteries of Osiris, Isis, and Horus, in Egypt; Atys and Cybéle, in Phrygia; Ceres and Proserpine, at Eleusis; of Venus and Adonis in Phœnicia; of Bona Dea, and Priapus, in Rome, are all susceptible of one explanation. They all set forth and illustrated, by solemn and impressive rites and mystical symbols, the grand phenomena of nature, especially as connected with the creation of things and the perpetuation of life. In all, it is

worthy of remark, the serpent was more or less conspicuously
introduced, always as symbolical of the invigorating or active
energy of nature.   In the mysteries of Ceres and Proserpine, the
grand secret communicated to the initiated was thus enigmatically
expressed: *Taurus Draconem genuit, et Taurum Draco*; " The
bull has begotten a serpent, and the serpent a bull.''   The bull,
as already seen, was a prominent emblem of generative force, the
Bacchus Zagreus, or Tauriformis.

The doctrine of an unending succession of forms was not
remotely connected with that of regeneration, or new birth, which
was part of the phallic system, and which was recognised in a
form more or less distinct in nearly all the primitive religions.
In Hindustan, this doctrine is still enforced in the most un-
equivocal manner, through the medium of rites of portentous
solemnity and significance to the devotees of the Hindu religion.
" For the purpose of regeneration,'' says Wilford, " it is directed
to make an image of pure gold of the female powers of nature in
the shape of either a woman or a cow.   In this statue the person
to be regenerated is enclosed, and afterwards dragged out through
the usual channel.   As a statue of pure gold, and of proper
dimensions would be too expensive, it is sufficient to make an
image of the sacred Yoni, through which the person to be regenerated is to pass.

We have seen the serpent as a symbol of productive energy
associated with the egg as a symbol of the passive elements of
nature.   The egg does not, however, appear except in the earlier
cosmogonies.   " As the male serpent,'' says Faber, "was employed to symbolize the Great Father, so the female serpent was
equally used to typify the Great Mother.   Such a mode of representation may be proved by express testimony, and is wholly
agreeable to the analogy of the entire system of Gentile mythology.
In the same manner that the two great parents were worshipped

under the hieroglyphics of a bull and cow, a lion and lioness, &c., so they were adored under the cognate figures of a male and female serpent."

Nearly every enquirer into the primitive superstitions of men has observed a close relationship, if not an absolute identity, in what are usually distinguished as Solar, Phallic, and Serpent Worship, yet the *rationale* of the connection has been rarely detected. They really are all forms of a single worship. " If (as it seems certain) they all three be identical," observes Mr. O'Brien, " where is the occasion for surprise at our meeting the sun, phallus, and serpent, the constituent symbols of each, occurring in combination, embossed upon the same table, and grouped upon the same architrave."

We turn again to America. The principal God of the Aztecs, subordinate to the great Unity, was the impersonation of the active, creative energy, Tezcatlipoca or Tonacatlecoatl. He was also called Tonacateuctli.

Like the Hindu Brahma, the Greek Phanes, and the Egyptian Phtha, he was the " Creator of heaven and earth," ·"the Great Father," " the God of Providence," who dwells in heaven, earth, and hades, and attends to the government of the world. To denote this unfailing power and eternal youth, his figure was that of a young man. His celestial emblem was Tonatiuh, the Sun. His companion or wife was Cihuacohuatl or Tonaeacihua, "the Great Mother " both of gods and men.

The remaining gods and goddesses of the Aztec Pantheon resolve themselves into modified impersonations of these two powers. Thus, we have Ometuctli and Omecihuatl, the adorable god and goddess who preside over the celestial paradise, and which, though generally supposed to be distinct divinities, are, nevertheless, according to the Codex Vaticanus, but other names for the deities already designated. We have also Xiuhteuctli,

" Master of the Year," " the God of Fire," the terrestrial symbol
of the active principle, and Xochitli, " the Goddess of Earth and
Corn ; " Tlaloc and Cinteotl, or Chalchiuhcue!je, " the god and
goddess of the waters ; " Mictlanteuctli and Mictlancihuatl, " the
god and goddess of the dead ; " the terrible Mexitli or Huitzlipochtli, corresponding to the Hindu Siva, in his character of
destroyer, and his wife Teoyamiqui, whose image, like that of
Kali, the consort of Siva, was decorated with the combined emblems of life and death.

In the simple mythology and pure Sabianism of Peru, we have
already shown the existence of the primeval principles symbolized, the first by the Sun and the second by his wife and sister
the Moon. That the sun was here regarded as symbolizing the
intermediate father, or demiurgic creator, cannot be doubted.
The great and solemn feast of Raimi was instituted in acknowledgment of the Sun as the great father of all visible things, by
whom all living things are generated and sustained. The ceremonies of this feast were emblematical, and principally referred
to the sun as the reproductive and preserving power of nature.
In Mexico, where the primitive religion partook of the fiercer
nature of the people, we find the Raimaic ceremonies assuming a
sanguinary character, and the acknowledgment of the reproductive associated with the propitiation of its antagonist principle,
as we see in the orgies of Huitzlipochtli in his character of the
Destroyer. The same remarks hold true of Central America, the
religion and mythology of which country correspond essentially
with those of the nations of Anahuac.

We have said that the principal god of the Aztec pantheon,
subordinate only to the Unity and corresponding to the Hindu
Brahma, was Tezcatlipoea, Tonacatlecoalt, or Tonacateuctli. If
we consult the etymology of these names we shall find ample
confirmation of the correctness of the deductions already drawn

from the mythologies of the East. Thus Tonacateuctli embodied Lord Sun from Tonàtiuh, Sun, *nacayo* or catl, body or person, and teuctli, master or lord. Again, Tonacatlcoatl, the Serpent Sun, from Tonctiah and catl, as above, and coatl, serpent. If we adopt another etymology for the names (and that which seems to have been most generally accepted by the early writers) we shall have Tonacateuctli, Lord of our Flesh, from to, the possessive pronoun plural, nacatl, flesh or body, and teuctli, master or lord. We shall also have Tonacatlecoatl, Serpent of our Flesh, from to, and nacatl, and coatl, serpent.

According to Sahagim, Tezcatlipoca, in his character of the God of Hosts, was addressed as follows by the Mexican High Priest:—" We entreat that those who die in war may be received by thee, our Father the Sun, and our Mother the Earth, for thou alone reignest." The same authority informs us that in the prayer of thanks, returned to Tezcatlipoca by the Mexican kings on the occasion of their coronation, God was recognised as the God of fire, to whom Xiuthteuctli, Lord of Vegetation, and specifically Lord of Fire, bears the same relation that Suyra does to the first person of the Hindu Triad. The king petitions that he may act "in conformity with the will of the ancient God, the Father of all Gods, who is the God of Fire; whose habitation is in the midst of the waters, encompassed by battlements, surrounded by rocks as it were with roses, whose name is Xiuteuctli,'' etc.

Tonacateuctli, or Tezcatlipoca, is often, not to say generally, both on the monuments and in the paintings, represented as surrounded by a disc of the sun.

The name of the primitive goddess, the wife of Tezcatlipoca, was Cihuacohuatl or Tonacacihua. She was well known by other names, all referring to her attributes. The etymology of Cihuacohuatl is clearly Cihua, woman or female, and coatl, serpent—Female Serpent. And Tonacacihua is Female Sun, from

Tonatiuh nacatl (as before) and cihua, woman or female. Adopting the other etymology, it is Woman of our Flesh.

Gama, who is said to be by far the most intelligent author who has treated with any detail of the Mexican Gods, referring to the serpent symbols belonging to the statue of Teoyaomiqui, says—" These refer to another Goddess named Cihuacohuatl, or Female Serpent, which the Mexicans believe gave to the light, at a single birth, two children, one male and the other female, to whom they refer the origin of mankind ; and hence twins, among the Mexicans, are called cohuatl or coatl, which is corrupted in the pronunciation by the vulgar into coate."

Whichever etymology we assign to Tonaca in these combinations, the leading fact that the Great Father was designated as the male serpent, and the Great Mother as the female serpent, remains unaffected. Not only were they thus designated, but Cinacoatl or Cihuacohuatl was generally if not always represented, in the paintings, accompanied by a great snake or feather-headed serpent (Tonacatlecoatl " serpent sun ") in which the monkish interpreters did not fail to discover a palpable allusion to Eve and the tempter of the garden.

Pursuing the subject of the connection of the Serpent Symbol with American Mythology, we remark the fact that it was a conspicuous symbol and could not escape the attention of the most superficial of observers of the Mexican and Central American monuments, and mythological paintings. The early Spaniards were particularly struck with its prominence.

" The snake," says Dupaix, " was a conspicuous object in the Mexican mythology, and we find it carved in various shapes and sizes, coiled, extended, spiral or entwined with great beauty, and sometimes represented with feathers and other ornaments. These different representatives," he continues, " no doubt denoted its different attributes."

The editor of Kingsborough's great work observes:—"Like the Egyptian Sphynx, the mystical snake of the Mexicans had its enigmas, and both are beyond our power to unravel;" this, however, is a matter of opinion, and the conclusion is one from which many will strongly dissent.

In almost every primitive mythology we find, not only a Great Father and Mother, the representatives of the reciprocal principles, and a Great Hermaphrodite Unity from whom the first proceed and in whom they are both combined, but we find also a beneficial character, partaking of a divine and human nature, who is the Great Teacher of Men, who instructs them in religion, civil organization and the arts, and who, after a life of exemplary usefulness, disappears mysteriously, leaving his people impressed with the highest respect for his institutions and the profoundest regard for his memory. This demi-god, to whom divine honours are often paid after his withdrawal from the earth, is usually the Son of the Sun, or of the Demiurgic Creator, the Great Father, who stands at the head of the primitive pantheons and subordinate only to the Supreme Unity; he is born of an earthly mother, a virgin, and often a vestal of the Sun, who conceives in a mysterious manner, and who, after giving birth to her half-divine son, is herself sometimes elevated to the rank of goddess. In the more refined and systematized mythologies he appears clearly as an incarnation of the Great Father and partaking of his attributes, his terrestrial representative, and the mediator between him and man. He appears as Buddha in India; Fohi in China; Schaka in Thibet; Zoroasta in Persia; Osiris in Egypt; Taut in Phœnicia; Hermes or Cadmus in Greece; Romulus in Rome; Odin in Scandinavia; and in each case is regarded as the Great Teacher of Men, and the founder of religion.

In the mythological systems of America, this intermediate demi-god was not less clearly recognised than in those of the Old World; indeed, as these systems were less complicated because less modified from the original or primitive forms, the Great Teacher appears here with more distinctness. Among the savage tribes his origin and character were, for obvious reasons, much confused; but among the more advanced nations he occupied a well-defined position.

Among the nations of Anahuac, he bore the name of Quetzalcoatl (Feathered Serpent) and was regarded with the highest veneration. His festivals were the most gorgeous of the year. To him it is said the great temple of Cholula was dedicated. His history, drawn from various sources, is as follows:— The god of the " Milky Way "— in other words, of Heaven—the principal deity of the Aztec Pantheon, and the Great Father of gods and men, sent a message to a virgin of Tulan, telling her that it was the will of the gods that she should conceive a son, which she did without knowing any man. This son was Quetzalcoatl, who was figured as tall, of fair complexion, open forehead, large eyes and a thick beard. He became high priest of Tulan, introduced the worship of the gods, established laws displaying the profoundest wisdom, regulated the calendar, and maintained the most rigid and exemplary manners in his life. He was averse to cruelty, abhorred war, and taught men to cultivate the soil, to reduce metal from their ores, and many other things necessary to their welfare. Under his benign administration the widest happiness prevailed amongst men. The corn grew to such a size that a single ear was a load for a man; gourds were as long as a man's body; it was unnecessary to dye cotton for it grew of all colours; all fruits were in the greatest profusion and of extraordinary size; there were also vast numbers of beautiful and sweet singing birds. His reign was the golden age of Anahuac. He however disappeared suddenly and mysteriously, in what manner is unknown. Some say he died on the sea-shore, and others say that he wandered away in search of the imaginary kingdom of Tlallapa. He was deified; temples were erected to him, and he was adored throughout Anahuac.

Quetzalcoatl is, therefore, but an incarnation of the " Serpent Sun " Tonacatlecoalt, and, as is indicated by his name, the feathered serpent was his recognised symbol. He was thus symbolized in accordance with a practice which (says Gama) prevailed in Mexico, of associating or connecting with the representatives of a god or goddess, the symbols of the other deities from whom they are derived, or to whom they sustain some relation. His temples were distinguished as being circular, and the one dedicated to his worship in Mexico, was, according to Gomera, entered by a door " like unto the mouth of a serpent, which was a thing to fear by those who went in thereat, especially by the Christians, to whom it represented very hell.''

The Mayas of Yucatan had a demi-god corresponding entirely with Quetzalcoatl, if he was not the same under a different name —a conjecture very well sustained by the evident relationship between the Mexican and Mayan mythologies. He was named Itzamna or Zamna, and was the only son of the principal God, Kinchanan. He arrived from the East, and instructed the people in all that was essential to their welfare. " He,'' says Cogolludo, " invented the characters which they use as letters, and which are called after him, Itzamna, and they adore him as a god.''

There was another similar character in Yucatan, called Ku Kulcan or Cuculcan, another in Nicaragua named Theotbilake, son of their principal god Thomathoyo, and another in Colombia bearing the name of Bochia. Peru and Guatemala furnish similar traditions, as do also Brazil, the nations of the Tamanac race, Florida, and various savage tribes of the West.

The serpent, as we show elsewhere, was an emblem both of Quetzalcoatl and of Ku Kulcan — a fact which gives some importance to the statement of Cabrera that Votan of Guatemala as above was represented to be a serpent, or of serpent origin.

Torquemada states that the images of Huitzlipochtli of Mexico, Quetzalcoatl, and Tlaloc were each represented with a golden serpent, bearing different symbolical sacrificial allusions. He also assures us that serpents often entered into the symbolical sacrificial ceremonies of the Mexicans, and presents the following example :—

" Among the many sacrifices which these Indians made, there was one which they performed in honour of the mountains, by forming serpents out of wood or of the roots of the trees, to which they affixed serpents' heads, and also dolls of the same, which they called Ecatotowin, which figures of serpents and fictitious children they covered with dough, named by them Tzoalli, composed of the seeds of Bledos, and placed them on supports of wood, carved in the representation of hills or mountains, on the tops of which they fixed them. This was the kind of offering which they made to the mountains and high hills.

The mother of Huitzlipochtli was a priestess of Tezcatlipoca (a cleanser of the temple, says Gama) named Coatlantona, Coatlcué, or Coatlcyue (serpent of the temple or serpent woman). She was extremely devoted to the gods, and one day when walking in the temple, she beheld, descending in the air, a ball made of variously coloured feathers. She placed it in her girdle, became at once pregnant, and afterwards was delivered of Mexith or Huitzlipochtli, full armed, with a spear in one hand, a shield in the other, and a crest of green feathers on his head. He became, according to some, their leader into Anahuac, guiding them to

place where Mexico is built. His statue was of gigantic size,
covered with ornaments each one of which had its significance.
was depicted placed upon a seat, from the four corners of
ch issued four large serpents. "His body," says Gomeza,
as beset with pearls, precious stones and gold, and for collars
chains around his neck ten hearts of men made of gold. It
also a counterfeit vizard, with eyes of glass, and in its neck
th painted, all of which things had their considerations and
nings." It was to him in his divine character of the destroyer
the bloodiest sacrifices of Mexico were performed. His wife,
yaomiqui (from Teo, sacred or divine; Yaoyotl, war; and
ui, to kill) was represented as a figure bearing the full breasts
woman, literally enveloped in serpents, and ornamented with
hers, shells, and the teeth and claws of a tiger. She had a
klace composed of six hands. Around her waist is a belt to
ch death's heads are attached. One of her statues, a horrible
re, still exists in the city of Mexico. It is carved from a
d block of basalt, and is nine feet in height and five and a
f in breadth.

It is not improbable that the serpent-mother of Huitzlipochtli
an impersonation of the great female serpent Cinacohuatl,
wife of Tonacatlecoatl, the serpent-father of Quetzalcoatl.
wever this may be, it is clear that a more intimate connection
sts between the several principal divinities of Mexico, than
ears from the confused and meagre accounts which have been
us of their mythology. Indeed, we have seen that the
ndu Triad, Brahma, Vishnu, and Siva, has very nearly its
interpart in Tezcatlipoca, Tlaloc, and the celestial Huitzli-
htli, the Creator, Preserver, and Destroyer and Reproducer.
the delineations of Siva or Mahadeo, in his character of the
troyer, he is represented as wrapped in tiger skins. A hooded
ke is twisted around him and lifts its head above his shoulder,

and twisted snakes form his head-dress. In other cases he holds a spear, a sword, a serpent, and a skull, and has a girdle of skulls around his waist. The bull Nandi (emblem of generative force), as also the lingham, are among his emblems. To him were dedicated the bloodiest sacrifices of India. Durga, or Kali (an impersonation of Bhavin, goddess of nature and fecundity) corresponds with the Mexican Tesyaomiqui, and is represented in a similar manner. She is a war goddess and her martial deeds give her a high position in the Hindu pantheon. As Kali, her representatives are most terrible. The emblems of destruction are common to all; she is entwined with serpents; a circlet of flowers surrounds her head; a necklace of skulls; a girdle of dissevered human hands; tigers crouching at her feet—indeed every combination of the horrible and the loathsome is invoked to portray the dark character which she represents. She delights in human sacrifices and the ritual prescribes that, previous to the death of the victim, she should be invoked as follows: " Let the sacrificer first repeat the name of Kali thrice, Hail, Kali! Kali! Hail, Devi! Hail, Goddess of Thunder! iron-sceptered, hail, fierce Kali! Cut, slay, destroy! bind, secure! Cut with the axe, drink blood, slay, destroy!" "She has four hands," says Patterson, "two of which are employed in the work of death; one points downwards, allusive to the destruction which surrounds her, and the other upwards, which seems to promise the regeneration of nature by a new creation. "On her festivals," says Coleman, "her temples literally stream with blood." As Durga, however, she is often represented as the patroness of Virtue and her battles with evil demons form the subject of many Hindu poems. She is under this aspect the armed Phallas.

We have seen that the Creator of the World, the Great Father of the Aztecs, Tonacatlecoatl or Tezcatlipoca, and his wife Cihuacohuatl, were not only symbolized as the Sun and

Moon, but also that they were designated as the male and female serpent, and that in the mythological pictures the former was represented as a feather-headed snake. We have also seen that the incarnate or human representative of this deity Quetzalcoatl, was also symbolized as a feathered serpent. This was in accordance with the system of the Aztecs, who represented cognate symbols, and invested the impersonations or descendants of the greater gods with their emblems.

These facts being well established, many monuments of American antiquity, otherwise inexplicable, become invested with significance. In Mexico, unfortunately, the monumental records of the ancient inhabitants have been so ruthlessly destroyed or obliterated that now they afford us but little aid in our researches. Her ancient paintings, although there are some which have escaped the general devastation, are principally beyond our reach and cannot be consulted particularly upon these points. In Central America, however, we find many remains which, although in a ruined state, are much more complete and much more interesting than any others concerning which we possess any certain information.

The researches and explorations of Messrs. Stephens and Catherwood have placed many of these before us in a form which enables us to detect their leading features. Ranking first among the many interesting groups of ruins discovered by these gentlemen, both in respect to their extent and character, are those of Chichen-itza. One of the structures comprising this group is described as follows:—" The building called the Castillo is the first which we saw, and is, from every point of view, the grandest and most conspicuous object that towers above the plain. The mound upon which it stands measures one hundred and ninety-seven feet at the base, and is built up, apparently solid, to the height of seventy-five feet. On the west side is a stair-way thirty-seven feet wide; on the north another, forty-four feet

wide, and containing ninety steps. On the ground at the fo
of the stairway, forming a bold, striking, and well-conceiv
commencement, are two colossal serpents' heads (feathered) t
feet in length, with mouths wide open and tongues protruding.

" No doubt they were emblematic of some religious belief, an
in the minds of the imaginative people passing between the
must have excited feelings of solemn awe. The platform on t
mound is about sixty feet square and is crowned by a buildi
measuring forty-three by forty-nine feet. Single doorways fa
the east, south and west, having massive lentils of zapote woc
covered with elaborate carvings, and the jambs are ornamen
with sculptured figures. The sculpture is much worn, but t
head-dress of feathers and portions of the rich attire still rema
The face is well preserved and has a dignified aspect. All t
other jambs are decorated with sculptures of the same gene
character, and all open into a corridor six feet wide, extendi
around three sides of the building. The interior of this buildi
was ornamented with very elaborate but much obliterat
carvings.

" The sacred character of this remarkable structure is a
parent at the first glance, and it is equally obvious that the vario
sculptures must have some significance. The entrance betwe
the two colossal serpents' heads remind us at once of Gomera
description of the entrance to the temple of Quetzalcoatl
Mexico, which ' was like unto the mouth of a serpent and whi
was a thing to fear by those who entered in thereat.' "

The circumstance that these heads are feathered seems furth
to connect this temple with the worship of that divinity. B
in the figures sculptured upon the jambs of the entrances, a
which, Mr. Stephens observes, were of the same general charac
throughout, we have further proof that this structure was ded
cated to a serpent divinity. Let it be remembered that t

dignified personage there represented is accompanied by a feathered serpent, the folds of which are gracefully arrayed behind the figure and the tail of which is marked by the rattles of the rattle-snake—the distinguishing mark of the monumental serpent of the continent, whether represented in the carvings of the mounds or in the sculptures of Central America. This temple, we may therefore reasonably infer, was sacred to the benign Quetzalcoatl, or a character corresponding to him, whose symbolical serpent guarded the ascent to the summit, and whose imposing representation was sculptured on its portals. This inference is supported by the fact that in Mexican paintings the temples of Quetzalcoatl are indicated by a serpent entwined around or rising above them, as may be seen in an example from the Codex Borgianus in Kingsborough.

But this is not all. We have already said that amongst the Itzaes—"holy men"—the founders of Chichen-itza and afterwards of Mayapan, there was a character, corresponding in many respects with Quetzalcoatl, named Ku Kulcan or Cuculcan. Torquemada, quoted by Cogolludo, asserts that this was but another name for Quetzalcoatl. Cogolludo himself speaks of Ku Kulcan as "one who had been a great captain among them," and was afterwards worshipped as a god. Herrara states that he ruled at Chichen-itza; that all agreed that he came from the westward, but that a difference exists as to whether he came before or afterwards or with the Itzaes. "But," he adds, "the name of the structure at Chichen-itza and the events of that country after the death of the lords, shows that Cuculcan governed with them. He was a man of good disposition, not known to have had wife or children, a great statesman, and therefore looked upon as a god, he having contrived to build another city in which business might be managed. To this purpose they pitched upon a spot eight leagues from Merida, where they made an enclosure of about an eighth of a league in circuit, being a wall of dry stone with only two gates. They built temples, calling the greatest of them Cuculcan. Near the enclosures were the houses of the prime men, among whom Cuculcan divided the land, appointing towns to each of them.

" This city was called Mayapan (the standard of Maya), the Mayan being the language of the country. Cuculcan governed in peace and quietness and with great justice for some years, when, having provided for his departure and recommended to them the good form of government which had been established, he returned to Mexico the same way he came, making some stay at Chanpotan, where, as a memorial of his journey, he erected a structure in the sea, which is to be seen to this day." *

We have here the direct statement that the principal structure at Mayapan was called Cuculcan; and from the language of Herrara the conclusion is irresistible that the principal structure of Chichen-itza was also called by the same name. These are extremely interesting facts, going far to show that the figure represented in the " Castillo," and which we have identified upon other evidence as being that of a personage corresponding to Quetzalcoatl, is none other than the figure of the demi-god Ku Kulcan, or Cuculcan, to whose worship the temple was dedicated and after whom it was named.

If we consult the etymology of the name Ku Kulcan we shall have further and striking evidence in support of this conclusion. *Ku* in the Mayan language means God, and *can* serpent. We have, then, Ku *Kul*can, God—*Kul*, Serpent, or Serpent-God. What *Kul* signifies it is not pretended to say, but we may reasonably conjecture that it is a qualifying word to *can* serpent. *Kukum* is feather, and it is possible that by being converted into an adjective form it may change its termination into Kukul. The etymology may therefore be Kukumcan Feather-Serpent, or

* Herrara, Hist. America, vol. iv., pp. 162-3.

Kukulcan Feathered Serpent. We, however, repose on the first explanation, and unhesitatingly hazard the opinion that, when opportunity is afforded of ascertaining the value of *Kul*, the correctness of our conclusions will be fully justified.

And here we may also add that the etymology of Kinchahan, the name of the principal god of the Mayas and corresponding to Tonacatlcoatl of Mexico, is precisely the same as that of the latter. *Kin* is Sun in the Mayan language, and *Chahan*, as every one acquainted with the Spanish pronunciation well knows, is nothing more than a variation in orthography for *Cüän* or *Can*, serpent. Kin Chahan, Kincaan, or Kincan is, therefore, Sun-serpent.

The observation that Quetzalcoatl might be regarded as the incarnation of Tezcatlipoca, or Tonacatlcoatl, corresponding to the Buddha of the Hindus, was based upon the coincidences in their origin, character, and teachings, but there are some remarkable coincidences between the temples dedicated to the worship of these two great teachers—or perhaps we should say, between the religious structures of Central America and Mexico and Hindustan and the islands of the Indian Archipelago, which deserve attention.

From the top of the lofty temple at Chichen-itza, just described, Mr. Stephens saw, for the first time, groups of columns or upright stones which, he observes, proved upon examination to be among the most remarkable and unintelligible remains he had yet encountered. " They stood in rows of three, four and five abreast, many rows continuing in the same direction, when they collectively changed and pursued another. They were low, the tallest not more than six feet high. Many had fallen, in some places lying prostrate in rows, all in the same direction, as if thrown intentionally. In some cases they extended to the bases of large mounds, on which were ruins of buildings and large

fragments of sculptures, while in others they branched off .
terminated abruptly. I counted three hundred and eighty, .
there were many more; but so many were broken and lay
irregularly that I gave up counting them."

Those represented by Mr. Stephens, in his plate, occur
immediate connection with the temple above described, .
enclose an area nearly four hundred feet square.

In the third volume of the " Transactions of the Royal Asia
Society " is an account of the mixed temples of the ancient
of Anarajapura (situated in the centre of the island of Ceyl
by Captain Chapman, of the British Army. The remarka
character of these ancient structures and the decided res
blances which they sustain to those of Central America, a
particularly to the group of Chichen-itza, justify a somew
detailed notice of them.

According to native records, Anarajapura was, for a perio
thirteen hundred years, both the principal seat of the religio
the country and the residence of its kings. It abounded
magnificent buildings, sculptures and other works of art, a
was, as it still is, held in the greatest veneration by the follow
of Buddha as the most sacred spot in the island.

" At this time," says Captain Chapman, " the only remain
traces of the city consist of nine temples; of two very extens
banks; of several smaller ones in ruins; of groups of pilla
and of portions of walls, which are scattered over an extent
several miles. The nine temples are still held in great reverer
and are visited periodically by the Buddhists. They consist f
of an enclosure, in which are the sacred trees called the Boga
the Thousand Pillars called Lowá Mahá Payá; and the se
mounds or Dagobas, each one of which has a distinct name gi
it by its founder."

The temple of Bo Malloa, especially sacred to Buddha, is
granite and consists of a series of four rectangular terraces, fa

with granite, rising out of each other and diminishing both in height and extent, upon which are situated the altars and the sacred Bogaha trees, or trees of Buddha. The total height of the terraces is about twenty feet and the extent of the largest thirty paces by fifteen. These terraces are ascended by flights of steps. At the foot of the principal flight are slabs of granite, placed perpendicularly, upon which figures are boldly sculptured; and between is a semi-circular stone with simple mouldings let in the ground. Upon the east of the building projects a colossal figure of Buddha. Another similar, but smaller, structure is placed a little to the eastward of that first described. Both are surrounded by a wall, enclosing a space one hundred and twenty-five paces long by seventy-five wide, within which are planted a variety of odoriferous trees.

A few paces to the eastward of this enclosure are the ruins of the "Thousand Pillars." These consisted originally of 1600 pillars, disposed in a square. The greater part are still standing; they consist, with a few exceptions, of a single piece of gneiss in the rough state in which they were quarried. They are ten or twelve feet above the ground; twelve inches by eight square, and about four feet from each other; but the two in the centre of the outer line differ from the rest in being of hard blue granite, and in being more carefully finished. These pillars were said to have been covered with *chunam* (plaster) and thus converted into columns having definite forms and proportions. There is a tradition that there was formerly in the centre of this square a brazen chamber, in which was contained a relic held in much veneration. A few paces from this was a single pillar of gneiss in a rough state, which was from fourteen to sixteen feet high.

Captain Chapman observes that structures, accompanied by similar groups of columns, exist on the opposite or continental coast. The temples of Rámiseram, Madura, and the celebrated

one of Seringham, have each their "Thousand Pillars." In
Rámiseram the pillars are arranged in colonnades of several
parallel rows, and these colonnades are separated by tanks or
spaces occupied by buildings in the manner indicated by Mr.
Stephens at Chichen-itza.   Some of these pillars are carved;
others are in their rough state or covered with plaster.   In
Madura the pillars are disposed in a square of lines radiating in
such a manner that a person placed in the centre can see through
in every direction.   This square is on a raised terrace, the pillars
rude and only about eight feet high.   At Seringham the pillars
also form a square.

The dagobas, occurring in connection with the temple of
Buddha and the "Thousand Pillars" at Anarájapura, deserve a
notice, as they correspond in many respects with some of the
structures at Chichen.   They are of various dimensions and consist generally of raised terraces or platforms of great extent,
surrounded by mounds of earth faced with brick or stone, and
often crowned with circular, dome-shaped structures.   The base
is usually surrounded by rows of columns.   They vary from
fifty to one hundred and fifty feet in height.   The dagobas, of
intermediate size, have occasionally a form approaching that of
a bubble, but in general they have the form of a bell.   They
constitute part of the Buddhist Temples, almost without exception.
We have, in the character of these singular columns and their
arrangement in respect to each other and the pyramidal
structures in connection with which they are found, a most striking resemblance between the ruins of Chichen-itza in Central
America, and Anarájapura in Ceylon—between the temples of
Buddha and those of Quetzalcoatl, or some corresponding
character.   The further coincidences which exist between the
sacred architecture of India and Central America will be reserved
for another place.   We cannot, however, omit to notice here the
structure at Chichen-itza designated as the "Caracol," both from

its resemblance to the dagobas of Ceylon and its connection with the worship of the Serpent Deity. Mr. Stephens describes it as follows:—

"It is circular in form and is known by the name of the Caracol, or Winding Staircase, on account of its interior arrangements. It stands on the upper of two terraces. The lower one measuring in front, from north to south, two hundred and twenty-three feet, and is still in good preservation. A grand staircase, forty-five feet wide, and containing twenty steps, rises to the platform of this terrace. On each side of the staircase, forming a sort of balustrade, rest the entwined bodies of two gigantic serpents, three feet wide, portions of which are still in place; and amongst the ruins of the staircase a gigantic head, which had terminated, at one side the foot of the steps. The platform of the second terrace measured eighty feet in front and fifty-five in depth, and is reached by another staircase forty-two feet wide and having forty-two steps. In the centre of the steps and against the wall of the terrace are the remains of a pedestal six feet high, on which probably once stood an idol. On the platform, fifteen feet from the last step, stands the building. It is twenty-two feet in diameter and has four small doorways facing the cardinal points. Above the cornice the roof sloped off so as to form an apex. The height, including the terraces, is little short of sixty feet. The doorways give entrance to a circular corridor five feet wide. The inner wall has four doorways, smaller than the others, and standing intermediately with respect to them. These doors give entrance to a second circular corridor, four feet wide, and in the centre is a circular mass, apparently of solid stone, seven feet six inches in diameter; but in one place, at the height of eleven feet from the floor, was a small square opening, which I endeavoured to clear out but without success. The roof was so tottering that I could not discover to what this opening led. The walls of both corridors were plastered and covered with paintings, and both were covered with a triangular arch.''

Mr. Stephens also found at Mayapan, which city, as we have seen, was built by Ku Kulcan, the great ruler and demi-god of Chichen-itza, a dome-shaped edifice of much the same character with that here described. It is the principal structure here, and stands on a mound thirty feet high. The walls are ten feet high to the top of the lower cornice, and fourteen more to the upper one. It has a single entrance towards the west. The outer wall is five feet thick, within which is a corridor three feet wide, surrounding a solid cylindrical mass of stone, nine feet in thickness. The walls have four or five coats of stucco and were covered with remains of paintings, in which red, yellow, blue and white were distinctly visible. On the south-west of the building was a double row of columns, eight feet apart, though probably from the remains around, there had been more, and by clearing away the trees others might be found. They were two feet and a half in diameter. We are not informed upon the point but presumably the columns were arranged, in respect to the structure, in the same manner as those accompanying the dagobas of Ceylon, or the mounds of Chichen-itza.

Among the ruins of Chichen are none more remarkable than that called by the natives " Egclesia '' or the Church. It is described by Mr. Stephens as consisting of " two immense parallel walls each two hundred and seventy-five feet long, thirty feet thick, and placed one hundred and twenty feet apart. One hundred feet from the northern extremity, facing the space between the walls, stands, on a terrace, a building thirty-five feet long, containing a single chamber, with the front fallen, and rising among the rubbish the remains of two columns elaborately ornamented, the whole interior wall being exposed to view, covered

from top to bottom with sculptured figures in bas-relief much
worn and faded. At the southern end also, placed back a hundred feet and corresponding in position, is another building
eighty-one feet long, in ruins, but also exhibiting the remains of
this column richly sculptured. In the centre of the great stone
walls, exactly opposite each other, and at the height of thirty feet
from the ground, are two massive stone rings, four feet in
diameter and one foot one inch thick, the diameter of the hole
is one foot seven inches. On the rim and border are sculptured
two entwined serpents; one of them is feather-headed, the other
is not." May we regard them as allusive to the Serpent God and
the Serpent Goddess of the Aztec mythology? Mr. Stephens is
disposed to regard the singular structure here described as a
Gymnasium or Tennis Court, and supports his opinion by a quotation from Herrara. It seems to others much more probable
that, with the other buildings of the group, this had an exclusively sacred origin. However that may be, the entwined serpents are clearly symbolical, inasmuch as we find them elsewhere,
in a much more conspicuous position, and occupying the first
place among the emblematic figures sculptured on the aboriginal
temples.

Immediately in connection with this singular structure and
constituting part of the eastern wall, is a building, in many respects the most interesting visited by Mr. Stephens, and respecting which it is to be regretted he has not given us a more complete
account. It requires no extraordinary effort of fancy to discover
in the sculptures and paintings with which it is decorated the
pictured records of the teachings of the deified Ku Kulcan, who
instructed men in the arts, taught them in religion, and instituted
government. There are represented processions of figures, covered
with ornaments, and carrying arms. "One of the inner cham-
bers is covered," says Mr. Stephens, "from the floor to the arched

roof, with designs in painting, representing, in bright and vivid
colours, human figures, battles, horses, boats, trees, and various
scenes in domestic life." These correspond very nearly with the
representations on the walls of the ancient Buddhist temples of
Java, which are described by Mr. Crawfurd as being covered
with designs of " a great variety of subjects, such as processions,
audiences, religious worship, battles, hunting, maritime, and
other scenes."

Among the ruins of Uxmal is a structure closely resembling
the Egclesia of Chichen. It consists of two massive walls of
stone, one hundred and twenty-eight feet long, and thirty in
thickness, and placed seventy feet apart. So far as could be
made out, they are exactly alike in plan and ornament. The
sides facing each other are embellished with sculpture, and upon
both remain the fragments of entwined colossal serpents which
run the whole length of the walls. In the centre of each facade,
as at Chichen, were the fragments of a great stone ring, which
had been broken off and probably destroyed. It would therefore
seem that the emblem of the entwined serpents was significant of
the purposes to which these structures were dedicated. The destruction of these stones is another evidence of their religious
character; for the conquerors always directed their destroying
zeal against those monuments, or parts of monuments, most
venerated and valued by the Indians, and which were deemed
most intimately connected with their superstitions.

Two hundred feet to the south of this edifice is another large
and imposing structure, called Casa de las Monjas, House of the
Nuns. It stands on the highest terraces, and is reached by a
flight of steps. It is quadrangular in form, with a courtyard in
the centre. This is two hundred and fourteen by two hundred
and fifty-eight. " Passing through the arched gateway," says
Mr. Stephens, " we enter this noble courtyard, with four great

facades looking down upon it, each ornamented from one end to
the other with the richest and most elaborate carving known in
the art of the builders. The facade on the left is most richly
ornamented, but is much ruined. It is one hundred and sixty
feet long, and is distinguished by two colossal serpents entwined,
running through and encompassing nearly all the ornaments
throughout its entire length. At the north end, where the facade
is most entire, the tail of one serpent is held up nearly over the
head of the other, and has an ornament upon it like a turban with
a plume of feathers. There are marks upon the extremity of the
tail, probably intended to represent the rattlesnake, with which
the country abounds. The lower serpent has its monstrous jaws
wide open, and within there is a human head, the face of which
is distinctly visible in the stone. The head and tail of the two
serpents at the south end of the facade are said to have corresponded with those at the north, and when the whole was entire,
in 1836, the serpents were seen encircling every ornament of the
building. The bodies of the serpents are covered with feathers.
Its ruins present a lively idea of the large and many well-con-
structed buildings of lime and stone, which Bernal Diaz saw at
Campeachy, with figures of serpents and idols painted on their
walls." Mr. Norman mentions that the heads of the serpents
were adorned with plumes of feathers, and that the tails showed
the peculiarity of the rattlesnake.*

The eastern facade, opposite that just described, is less
elaborately, but more tastefully ornamented. Over each doorway is an ornament representing the Sun. In every instance
there is a face in the centre, with the tongue projected, surmounted by an elaborate head-dress; between the bars there is
also a range of many lozenge-shaped ornaments, in which the
remains of red paint are distinctly visible, and at each end is a
serpent's head with the mouth open. The ornament over the

* Trav. in Yucatan.

principal doorway is much more complicated and elaborate, and
of that marked and peculiar style which characterizes the highest
efforts of the builders.

The central figure, with the projecting tongue, is probably
that of the Sun, and in general design coincides with the central
figure sculptured on the great calendar stone of Mexico, and with
that found by Mr. Stephens on the walls of Casa No. 3 at
Palenque, where it is represented as an object of admiration.
The protrusion of the tongue signified, among the Aztecs, ability
to speak, and denoted life or existence. Among the Sclavonian
nations, the idea of vitality was conveyed by ability to eat, as it
is by to breathe among ourselves, and to walk among the Indians
of the Algonquin stock.

Although Central America was occupied by nations independent of those of Mexico proper, yet some of them (as those in-
habiting the Pacific coast, as far south as Nicaragua) were
descended directly from them, and all had striking features in
common with them. Their languages were in general different,
but cognate; their architecture was essentially the same; and
their religion, we have every reason for believing, was not widely
different, though doubtless that of the south was less ferocious
in its character, and not so generally disfigured by human
sacrifices.

We may therefore look with entire safety for common mythological notions, especially when we are assured of the fact that,
whatever its modifications, the religion of the continent is
essentially the same; and especially when we know that whatever
differences may have existed amongst the various nations of
Mexico and Central America, the elements of their religion were
derived from a common Tottecan root.

CHAPTER VI.

*Mexican Temple of Montezuma—The Serpent Emblem in Mexico—
Pyramid of Cholula—Tradition of the Giants of Anahuac—The
Temple of Quetzalcoatl—North American Indians and the Rattle-
snake—Indian Tradition of a Great Serpent—Serpents in the
Mounds of the West—Bigotry and Folly of the Spanish Conquerors
of the West—Wide prevalence of Mexican Ophiolatreia.*

THE monuments of Mexico representing the serpent are very
numerous, and have been specially remarked by nearly
every traveller in that interesting country. The symbol is equally
conspicuous in the ancient paintings.

"The great temple of Mexico," says Acosta, "was built of
great stones in fashion of snakes tied one to another, and the
circuit was called coate-pantli which is circuit of snakes." Duran
informs us that this temple was expressly built by the first Montezuma "for all the gods," and hence called Coatlan, literally
"serpent place." It contained, he also informed us, the temple
or shrine of Tezcatlipoca, Huitzlipochtli, and Tlaloc, called
Coateocalli, "Temple of the Serpent."

Says Bernal Diaz, in his account of the march of Cortes to
Mexico, "We to-day arrived at a place called Terraguco, which
we called the town of the serpents, on account of the enormous
figures of those reptiles which we found in their temples, and
which they worshipped as gods."

It cannot be supposed that absolute serpent worship—a simple
degraded adoration of the reptile itself, or Fetishism, such as is
said to exist in some parts of Africa—prevailed in Mexico. The
serpent entered into their religious systems only as an emblem.
It is nevertheless not impossible, on the contrary it is extremely
probable, that a degree of superstitious veneration attached to the
reptile itself. According to Bernal Diaz, living rattlesnakes were

kept in the great temple of Mexico as sacred objects. He says, "Moreover, in that accursed house they kept vipers and venomous snakes, who had something at their tails which sounded like morris-bells, and these are the worst of vipers. They were kept in cradles and barrels, and in earthen vessels, upon feathers, and there they laid their eggs, and nursed up their snakelings, and they were fed with the bodies of the sacrificed, and with dogs' meat."

Charlevaix in the History of Paraguay, relates "that Alvarez, in one of his expeditions into that country, found a town in which was a large tower or temple the residence of a monstrous serpent which the inhabitants had chosen for a divinity and which they fed with human flesh. He was as thick as an ox, and seven and twenty feet long." This account has been regarded as somewhat apocryphal, although it is likely enough that Serpent Worship may have existed among some of the savage tribes of South America.

It has been said "it should be remarked that Diaz was little disposed to look with complacency upon the religion of the Mexicans, or whatever was connected with it, and that his prejudices were not without their influence on his language. His relation, nevertheless, may be regarded as essentially reliable."

Mr. Mayer, in his Description of Mexico, gives an interesting account of the ancient and extraordinary Indian Pyramid of Cholula, an erection intimately connected with the Quetzalcoatl we have been speaking of.

This is one of the most remarkable relics of the aborigines on the continent, for, although it was constructed only of the adobes or common sun-dried brick, it still remains in sufficient distinctness to strike every observer with wonder at the enterprise of its Indian builders. What it was intended for, whether tomb or temple, no one has determined with certainty, though the wisest antiquarians have been guessing since the conquest. In the midst of a plain the Indians erected a mountain. The base still remains to give us its dimensions; but what was its original height? Was it the tomb of some mighty lord, or sovereign prince; or was it alone a place of sacrifice?

Many years ago in cutting a new road toward Puebla from Mexico it became necessary to cross a portion of the base of this pyramid. The excavation laid bare a square chamber, built of stone, the roof of which was sustained by cypress beams. In it were found some idols of basalt, a number of painted vases, and the remains of two dead bodies. No care was taken of these relics by the discoverers, and they are lost to us for ever.

Approaching the pyramid from the east, it appears so broken and overgrown with trees that it is difficult to make out any outline distinctly. From the west, however, a very fair idea may be obtained of this massive monument as it rises in solitary grandeur from the midst of the wide-spreading plain. A well-paved road cut by the old Spaniards, ascends from the north-west corner with steps at regular intervals, obliquing first on the west side to the upper bench of the terrace, and thence returning toward the same side until it is met by a steep flight rising to the front of the small dome-crowned chapel, surrounded with its grave of cypress and dedicated to the Virgin of Remedies.

The summit is perfectly level, and protected by a parapet wall, whence a magnificent view extends on every side over the level valley. Whatever this edifice may have been, the idea of thus attaining permanently an elevation to which the people might resort for prayer—or even for parade or amusement—was a sublime conception and entitles the men who, centuries ago, patiently erected the lofty pyramid, to the respect of posterity.

There remain at present but four stories of the Pyramid of Cholula, rising above each other and connected by terraces.

These stones are formed, as already said, of sun-dried bricks, interspersed with occasional layers of plaster and stone work. "And this is all," says Mr. Mayer, "that is to be told or described. Old as it is—interesting as it is—examined as it has been by antiquaries of all countries—the result has ever been the same. The Indians tell you that it was a place of sepulture, and the Mexicans give you the universal reply of ignorance in this country: *Quien Sabe?*—who knows? who can tell?"

Baron Humboldt says:—" The Pyramid of Cholula is exactly the same height as that of Tonatiuh Ylxaqual, at Teotihuacan. It is three metres higher than that of Mycerinus, or the third of the great Egyptian pyramids of the group of Djizeh. Its base, however, is larger than that of any pyramid hitherto discovered by travellers in the old world, and is double of that known as the Pyramid of Cheops. Those who wish to form an idea of the immense mass of this Mexican monument by the comparison of objects best known to them, may imagine a square four times greater than that of the Place Vendôme in Paris, covered with layers of bricks rising to twice the elevation of the Louvre. Some persons imagine that the whole of the edifice is not artificial, but as far as explorations have been made there is no reason to doubt that it is entirely a work of art. In its present state (and we are ignorant of its perfect original height) its perpendicular proportion is to its base as eight to one, while in the three great pyramids of Djizeh the proportion is found to be one and six-tenths to one and seven-tenths to one; or nearly as eight to five."

May not this have been the base of some mighty temple destroyed long before the conquest, and of which even the tradition no longer lingers among the neighbouring Indians?

In continuation Humboldt observes "that the inhabitants of Anahuac apparently designed giving the Pyramid of Cholula the same height, and double the base of the Pyramid of Teotihuacan, and that the Pyramid of Asychis, the largest known of the

gyptian, has a base of 800 feet, and is like that of Cholula
uilt of brick. The cathedral of Strasburg is eight feet, and the
oss of St. Peter's at Rome forty-one feet lower than the top
the Pyramid of Cheops. Pyramids exist throughout Mexico;
. the forests of Papantla at a short distance above the level of
e sea; on the plains of Cholula and of Teotihuacan, at the
evations which exceed those of the passes of the Alps. In the
ost widely distant nations, in climates the most different, man
ems to have adopted the same style of construction, the same
naments, the same customs, and to have placed himself under
e government of the same political institutions."

Is this an argument? it has been asked; that all men have
rung from one stock, or that the human mind is the same
erywhere, and, affected by similar interests or necessities,
variably comes to the same result, whether pointing a pyramid
· an arrow, in making a law or a ladle?

"Much as I distrust," says Mayer, " all the dark and groping
forts of antiquarians, I will nevertheless offer you some sketches
1d legends which may serve at least to base a conjecture upon
; to the divinity to whom this pyramid was erected, and to
·ove, perhaps, that it was intended as the foundation of a temple
1d not the covering of a tomb."

A tradition, which has been recorded by a Dominican monk
10 visited Cholula in 1566, is thus related from his work, by
e traveller already quoted.

"Before the great inundation which took place 4,800 years
ter the erection of the world, the country of Anahuac was in-
.bited by giants, all of whom either perished in the inundation
were transformed into fishes, save seven who fled into caverns.

" When the waters subsided, one of the giants, called Xelhua,
rnamed the ' Architect,' went to Cholula, where as a memorial
the Tlaloc which had served for an asylum to himself and his

G

six brethren, he built an artificial hill in the form of a pyramid.
He ordered bricks to be made in the province of Tlalmanalco, at
the foot of the Sierra of Cecotl, and in order to convey them to
Cholula he placed a file of men who passed them from hand to
hand.   The gods beheld, with wrath, an edifice the top of which
was to reach the clouds.   Irritated at the daring attempt of
Xelhua, they hurled fire on the pyramid.   Numbers of the work-
men perished.   The work was discontinued, and the monument
was afterwards dedicated to Quetzalcoatl.''   Of this god we have
already given a description in these pages.

The following singular story in relation to this divinity and
certain services of his temple, is to be found in the "Natural and
Moral History of Acosta," book 5, chap. 30.

" There was at this temple of Quetzalcoatl, at Cholula, a court
of reasonable greatness, in which they made great dances and
pastimes with games and comedies, on the festival day of this
idol, for which purpose there was in the midst of this court a
theatre of thirty feet square, very finely decked and trimmed—
the which they decked with flowers that day—with all the art
and invention that might be, being environed around with arches
of divers flowers and feathers, and in some places there were tied
many small birds, conies, and other tame beasts.   After dinner,
all the people assembled in this place, and the players presented
themselves and played comedies.   Some counterfeited the deaf
and rheumatic, others the lame, some the blind and crippled
which came to seek for cure from the idol.   The deaf answered
confusedly, the rheumatic coughed, the lame halted, telling their
miseries and griefs, wherewith they made the people to laugh.
Others came forth in the form of little beasts, some attired like
snails, others like toads, and some like lizards; then meeting
together they told their offices, and, everyone retiring to his place
they sounded on small flutes which was pleasant to hear.   The

likewise counterfeited butterflies and small birds of divers colours which were represented by the children who were sent to the temple for education. Then they went into a little forest, planted there for the purpose, whence the priests of the temple drew them forth with instruments of music. In the meantime they used many pleasant speeches, some in propounding, others in defending, wherewith the assistants were pleasantly entertained. This done, they made a masque or mummery with all the personages, and so the feast ended."

From these traditions we derive special important facts. that Quetzalcoatl was "god of the air;" second, that he was represented as a "feathered serpent;" third, that he was the great divinity of the Cholulans; and fourth, that a hill was raised by them upon which they erected a temple to his glory where they celebrated his festivals with pomp and splendour.

Combining all these, is it unreasonable to believe that the Pyramid of Cholula was the base of this temple, and that he was there worshipped as the Great Spirit of the Air—or of the seasons; the God who produced the fruitfulness of the earth, regulated the Sun, the wind, and the shower, and thus spread plenty over the land. It has been thought too, that the serpent might not improbably typify lightning, and the feathers swiftness, thus denoting one of the attributes of the air—and that the most speedy and destructive.

Mr. Mayer says:—" I constantly saw serpents, in the city of Mexico, carved in stone, and in the various collections of antiquities," and he gives drawings of several of the principal, notably one carved with exquisite skill and found in the court-yard of the University.

Vasquez Coronado, Governor of New Gallicia, as the northern territories of Spain were then called, wrote to the Viceroy Mendoza in 1539, concerning the unknown regions still beyond him .

to the northward. His account was chiefly based upon the fabulous relation of the Friar Marco Niza, and is not entirely to be relied upon. In this letter he mentions that " in the province of Topira there were people who had great towers and temples covered with straw, with small round windows, filled with human skulls, and before the temple a great round ditch, the brim of which was compassed with a serpent, made of various metals, which held its tail in its mouth, and before which men were sacrificed."

Du Paix has given many examples of the carving representing the snake, which he found in his Antiquarian Explorations in Mexico. One found near the ancient city of Chochimilco represents a snake artificially coiled carved from a block of porphry. " Its long body is gracefully entwined, leaving its head and tail free. There is something showy in the execution of the figure. Its head is elevated and curiously ornamented, its open mouth exhibits two long and pointed fangs, its tongue (which is unusually long) is cloven at the extremity like an anchor, its body is fancifully scaled, and its tail (covered with circles) ends with three rattles. The snake was a frequent emblem with the Mexican artists. The flexibility of its figure rendering it susceptible of an infinite diversity of position, regular and irregular; they availed themselves of this advantage and varied their representations of it without limit and without ever giving it an unnatural attitude."

Near Quauhquechúla, Du Paix found another remarkable sculpture of the serpent carved in black basalt, and so entwined that the space within the folds of its body formed a font sufficiently large to contain a considerable quantity of water. The body of the reptile was spirally entwined, and the head probably served as a handle to move it. It was decorated with circles, and the tail was that of a rattlesnake.

Du Paix also found at Tepeyaca, in a quarter of the town called St. Michael Tlaixegui (signifying in the Mexican language the cavity of the mountain) a serpent carved in red porphry. It is of large dimensions, in an attitude of repose, and coiled upon itself in spiral circles so as to leave a hollow space or transverse axis in the middle.   The head, which has a fierce expression, is armed with two long and sharp fangs, and the tongue is double being divided longitudinally.   The entire surface of the body is ornamented or covered with broad and long feathers, and the tail terminates in four rattles.   Its length from the head to the extremity of the tail is about twenty feet, and it gradually diminishes in thickness. " This reptile," Du Paix says, " was the monarch or giant of its species, and in pagan times was a deity greatly esteemed under the name Quetzalcoatl, or Feathered Serpent.   It is extremely well sculptured, and there are still marks of its having been once painted with vermillion."

But the symbolical feathered serpent was not peculiar to Mexico and Yucatan.   Squier, in his Explorations in Nicaragua, several times encountered it.   Near the city of Santiago de Managua, the capital of the Republic, situated upon the shores of Lake Managua or Leon, and near the top of the high volcanic ridge which separates the .waters flowing into the Atlantic from those running into the Pacific, is an extinct crater, now partially filled with water, forming a lake nearly two miles in circumference, called Nihapa.   The sides of this crater are perpendicular rocks ranging from five hundred to eight hundred feet in height. There is but one point where descent is possible.   It leads.to a little space, formed by the fallen rocks and debris which permits a foothold for the traveller.   Standing here, he sees above him, on the smooth face of the cliff, a variety of figures, executed by the aborigines, in red paint.   Most conspicuous amongst them, is a feathered serpent coiled and ornamented.   It is about four feet in diameter. Upon some of the other rocks were found paintings of the serpent, perfectly corresponding with the representations in the Dresden MS. copied by Kingsborough and confirming the conjectures of Humboldt and other investigators that this MS. had its origin to the southward of Mexico. The figure copied was supposed by the natives who had visited it to represent the sun. Some years ago, large figures of the sun and moon were visible upon the cliffs, but the section upon which they were painted was thrown down by the great earthquake of 1838. Parts of the figures can yet be traced upon the fallen fragments.

It is a singular fact that many of the North American Indian tribes entertain a superstitious regard for serpents, and particularly for the rattlesnake. Though always avoiding, they never destroyed it, "lest," says Bartram, "the spirit of the reptile should excite its kindred to revenge."

According to Adair, this fear was not unmingled with veneration. Charlevoix states that the Natchez had the figure of a rattlesnake, carved from wood, placed among other objects upon the altar of their temple, to which they paid great honours. Heckwelder relates that the Linni Linape, called the rattlesnake "grandfather" and would on no account allow it to be destroyed. Henney states that the Indians around Lake Huron had a similar superstition, and also designated the rattlesnake as their "grandfather." He also mentions instances in which offerings of tobacco were made to it, and its parental care solicited for the party performing the sacrifice. Carver also mentions an instance of similar regard on the part of a Menominee Indian, who carried a rattlesnake constantly with him, "treating it as a deity, and calling it his great father."

A portion of the veneration with which the reptile was regarded in these cases may be referred to that superstition so common among the savage tribes, under the influence of which

everything remarkable in nature was regarded as a medicine or
mystery, and therefore entitled to respect. Still there appears to
be, linked beneath all, the remnant of an Ophite superstition of
a different character which is shown in the general use of the
serpent as a symbol of incorporeal powers, of " Manitous " or
spirits.

Mr. James, in his MSS. in the possession of the New York
Historical Society, states, " that the Menominees translate the
manitou of the Chippeways by *akwahtoke*," which means em-
phatically a snake. " Whether," he continues, " the word was
first formed as a name for a surprising or disgusting object, and
thence transferred to spiritual beings, or whether the extension of
its signification has been in an opposite direction, it is difficult
to determine.'' Bossu also affirms that the Arkansas believed in
the existence of a great spirit, which they adore under form of a
serpent. In the North-west it was a symbol of evil power.

Here we may suitably introduce the tradition of a great serpent, which is to this day current amongst a large portion of the
Indians of the Algonquin stock. It affords some curious
parallelisms with the allegorical relations of the old world. The
Great Teacher of the Algonquins, Manabozho, is always placed in
antagonism to a great serpent, a spirit of evil, who corresponds
very nearly with the Egyptian Typhon, the Indian Kaliya, and
the Scandinavian Midgard. He is also connected with the Algonquin notions of a deluge; and as Typhon is placed in opposition
to Osiris or Apollo, Kaliya to Surya or the Sun, and Midgard to
Wodin or Odin, so does he bear a corresponding relation to Manabozho. The conflicts between the two are frequent; and although
the struggles are sometimes long and doubtful, Manabozho is
usually successful against his adversary. One of these contests
involved the destruction of the earth by water, and its reproduction by the powerful and beneficent Manabozho. The tradition

in which this grand event is embodied was thus related by Kah-ge-ga-gah-boowh, a chief of the Ojibway.   In all of its essentials, it is recorded by means of the rude pictured signs of the Indians, and scattered all over the Algonquin territories.

One day returning to his lodge, from a long journey, Mana-bozho missed from it his young cousin, who resided with him, he called his name aloud, but received no answer.   He looked around on the sand for the tracks of his feet, and he there, for the first time, discovered the trail of Meshekenabek, the serpent. He then knew that his cousin had been seized by his great enemy.   He armed himself, and followed on his track, he passed the great river, and crossed mountains and valleys to the shores of the deep and gloomy lake now called Manitou Lake, Spirit Lake, or the Lake of Devils.   The trail of Meshekenabek led to the edge of the water.

At the bottom of this lake was the dwelling of the serpent, and it was filled with evil spirits—his attendants and companions. Their forms were monstrous and terrible, but most, like their master, bore the semblance of serpents.   In the centre of this horrible assemblage was Meshekenabek himself, coiling his volumes around the hapless cousin of Manabozho.   His head was red as with blood, and his eyes were fierce and glowed like fire.   His body was all over armed with hard and glistening scales of every shade and colour.

Manabozho looked down upon the writhing spirits of evil, and he vowed deep revenge.   He directed the clouds to disappear from the heavens, the winds to be still, and the air to become stagnant over the lake of the manitous, and bade the sun shine upon it with all its fierceness; for thus he sought to drive his enemy forth to seek the cool shadows of the trees, that grew upon its banks, so that he might be able to take vengeance upon him.

Meanwhile, Manabozho seized his bow and arrows and placed himself near the spot where he deemed the serpents would come to enjoy the shade. He then transferred himself into the broken stump of a withered tree, so that his enemies might not discover his presence.

The winds became still, and the sun shone hot on the lake of the evil manitous. By and by the waters became troubled, and bubbles rose to the surface, for the rays of the sun penetrated to the horrible brood within its depths. The commotion increased, and a serpent lifted its head high above the centre of the lake and gazed around the shores. Directly another came to the surface, and they listened for the footsteps of Manabozho but they heard him nowhere on the face of the earth, and they said one to the other, "Manabozho sleeps." And then they plunged again beneath the waters, which seemed to hiss as they closed over them.

It was not long before the lake of manitous became more troubled than before, it boiled from its very depths, and the hot waves dashed wildly against the rocks on its shores. The commotion increased, and soon Meshekenabek, the Great Serpent, emerged slowly to the surface, and moved towards the shore. His blood-red crest glowed with a deeper hue, and the reflection from his glancing scales was like the blinding glitter of a sleet covered forest beneath the morning sun of winter. He was followed by the evil spirits, so great a number that they covered the shores of the lake with their foul trailing carcases.

They saw the broken, blasted stump into which Manabozho had transformed himself, and suspecting it might be one of his disguises, for they knew his cunning, one of them approached, and wound his tail around it, and sought to drag it down. But Manabozho stood firm, though he could hardly refrain from crying aloud, for the tail of the monster tickled his sides.

The Great Serpent wound his vast folds among the trees of
the forest, and the rest also sought the shade, while one was left
to listen for the steps of Manabozho.

When they all slept, Manabozho silently drew an arrow from
his quiver, he placed it in his bow, and aimed it where he saw the
heart beat against the sides of the Great Serpent. He launched
it, and with a howl that shook the mountains and startled the
wild beasts in their caves, the monster awoke, and, followed by
its frightful companions, uttering mingled sounds of rage and
terror, plunged again into the lake. Here they vented their fury
on the helpless cousin of Manabozho, whose body they tore into a
thousand fragments, his mangled lungs rose to the surface, and
covered it with whiteness. And this is the origin of the foam on
the water.

When the Great Serpent knew that he was mortally wounded,
both he and the evil spirits around him were rendered tenfold
more terrible by their great wrath and they rose to overwhelm
Manabozho. The water of the lake swelled upwards from its
dark depths, and with a sound like many thunders, it rolled
madly on its track, bearing the rocks and trees before it with
resistless fury. High on the crest of the foremost wave, black as
the midnight, rode the writhing form of the wounded Meshekenabek, and red eyes glazed around him, and the hot breaths of the
monstrous brood hissed fiercely above the retreating Manabozho.
Then thought Manabozho of his Indian children, and he ran by
their villages, and in a voice of alarm bade them flee to the
mountains, for the Great Serpent was deluging the earth in his
expiring wrath, sparing no living thing. The Indians caught up
their children, and wildly sought safety where he bade them.
But Manabozho continued his flight along the base of the western
hills, and finally took refuge on a high mountain beyond Lake
Superior, for towards the north. There he found many men and

animals who had fled from the flood that already covered the valleys and plains, and even the highest hills. Still the waters continued to rise, and soon all the mountains were overwhelmed save that on which stood Manabozho. Then he gathered together timber, and made a raft, upon which the men and women, and the animals that were with him, all placed themselves. No sooner had they done so, than the rising floods closed over the mountain and they floated alone on the surface of the waters; and thus they floated for many days, and some died, and the rest became sorrowful, and reproached Manabozho that he did not disperse the waters and renew the earth that they might live. But though he knew that his great enemy was by this time dead, yet could not Manabozho renew the world unless he had some earth in his hands wherewith to begin the work. And this he explained to those that were with him, and he said that were it ever so little, even a few grains of earth, then could he disperse the waters and renew the world. Then the beaver volunteered to go to the bottom of the deep, and get some earth, and they all applauded her design. She plunged in, they waited long, and when she returned she was dead; they opened her hands but there was no earth in them. "Then," said the otter, "will I seek the earth:" and the bold swimmer dived from the raft. The otter was gone still longer than the beaver, but when he returned to the surface he too was dead, and there was no earth in his claws. "Who shall find the earth?" exclaimed all those left on the raft, "now that the beaver and the otter are dead?" and they desponded more than before, repeating, "Who shall find the earth?" "That will I," said the muskrat, and he quickly disappeared between the logs of the raft. The muskrat was gone very long, much longer than the otter, and it was thought he would never return, when he suddenly rose near by, but he was too weak to speak, and he swam slowly towards the raft. He had hardly got

upon it when he too died from his great exertion.   They opened
his little hands and there, clasped closely between the fingers,
they found a few grains of fresh earth.   These Manabozho carefully collected and dried them in the sun, and then he rubbed
them into a fine powder in his palms, and, rising up, he blew
them abroad upon the waters.   No sooner was this done than the
flood began to subside, and soon the trees on the mountains and
hills emerged from the deep, and the plains and the valleys came
in view and the waters disappeared from the land leaving no trace
but a thick sediment, which was the dust that Manabozho had
blown abroad from the raft.

Then it was found that Meshekenabek, the Great Serpent, was
dead, and that the evil manitous, his companions, had returned to
the depths of the lake of spirits, from which, for the fear of
Manabozho, they never more dared to come forth.   And in
gratitude to the beaver, the otter, and the muskrat, those animals
were ever after held sacred by the Indians, and they became their
brethren, and they never killed nor molested them until the
medicine of the stranger made them forget their relations and
turned their hearts to ingratitude.

In the mounds of the West have been found various sculptures
of the serpent, and amongst them one as follows:—It represents
a coiled rattlesnake, and is carved in a very compact cinnamon-
coloured sandstone.   It is six and a quarter inches long, one and
three-eighths broad, and a quarter of an inch thick.   The workmanship is delicate, and the characteristic features of the rattlesnake are perfectly represented; the head, unfortunately, is not
entire, but enough remains to show that it was surmounted by
some kind of feather-work resembling that so conspicuously represented in the sculptured monuments of the South.   It was found
carefully enveloped in sheet copper, and under circumstances
which render it certain that it was an object of high regard and
probably of worship.

Notwithstanding the striking resemblances which have been pointed out, in the elementary religions of the old and new worlds, and the not less remarkable coincidences in their symbolical systems, we are scarcely prepared to find in America that specific combination which fills so conspicuous a place in the early cosmogonies and mythologies of the East, and which constitute the basis of these investigations, namely, the compound symbol of the Serpent and the Egg. It must be admitted that, in the few meagre and imperfect accounts which we have of the notions of cosmogony entertained by the American nations, we have no distinct allusion to it. The symbolism is far too refined and abstract to be adopted by wandering, savage tribes, and we can only look for it, if at all, among the more civilized nations of the central part of the continent, where religion and mythology ranked as an intelligible system.   And here we have at once to regret and reprobate the worse than barbarous zeal of the Spanish conquerors, who, not content with destroying the pictured records and over-turning and defacing the primitive monuments of those remarkable nations; distorted the few traditions which they recorded, so as to lend a seeming support to the fictions of their own religion, and invested the sacred rites of the aborigines with horrible and repulsive features, so as to furnish, among people like minded with themselves, some apology for their savage cruelty.   Not only were orders given by the first Bishop of Mexico, the infamous Zumanaga, for the burning of all the Mexican MSS. which could be procured, but all persons were discouraged from recording the traditions of the ancient inhabitants.

So far, therefore, from having a complete and consistent account of the beliefs and conceptions of those nations, to which reference may be had in inquiries of this kind, we have only detached and scattered fragments, rescued by later hands from the general destruction.   Under such circumstances we cannot expect to find parallel evidences of the existence of specific conceptions; that is to say, we may find certain representations clearly symbolical and referring to the cosmogony, mythology, or religion of the primitive inhabitants and yet look in vain among the scanty and distorted traditions and few mutilated pictured records which are left us for collateral support of the significance which reason and analogy may assign to them.

It is not assumed to say that any distinct representation of the Serpent and the Egg exists amongst the monuments of Mexico or Central America; what future investigations may disclose remains to be seen. If, until the present time, we have remained in profound ignorance of the existence of the grand monument under notice, in one of the best populated states, what treasures of antiquity may yet be hidden in the fastnesses of the central part of the continent!

It has often been said that every feature in the religion of the New World, discovered by Cortez and Pizarro, indicates an origin common to the superstitions of Egypt and Asia. The same solar worship, the same pyramidal monuments, and the same Ophiolatreia distinguish them all.

Acosta says "the temple of Vitziliputzli was built of great stones in fashion of snakes tied one to another, and the circuit was called ' the circuit of snakes ' because the walls of the enclosure were covered with the figures of snakes. Vitziliputzli held in his right hand a staff cut in the form of a serpent, and the four corners of the ark in which he was seated terminated each with a carved representation of the head of a serpent. The Mexican century was represented by a circle, having the sun in the centre, surrounded by the symbols of the years. The circumference was a serpent twisted into four knots at the cardinal points." *

The Mexican month was divided into twenty days; the serpent and dragon symbolised two of them. In Mexico there was also a temple dedicated to the God of the Air, and the door of it was formed so as to resemble a serpent's mouth.[*]

Amongst other things, Peter Martyr mentions a large serpent-idol at Campeachy, made of stones and bitumen, in the act of devouring a marble lion. When first seen by the Spaniards it was warm with the blood of human victims.

" Ancient painting and sculptures abound with evidences of Mexican Ophiolatreia, and prove that there was scarcely a Mexican deity who was not symbolized by a serpent or a dragon. Many deities appear holding serpents in their hands, and small figures of priests are represented with a snake over each head. This reminds us forcibly of the priests of the Egyptian Isis, who are described in sculpture with the sacred asp upon the head and a cone in the left hand. And to confirm the original mutual connexion of all the serpent-worshippers throughout all the world — the Mexican paintings, as well as the Egyptian and Persian hieroglyphics, describe the Ophite Hierogram of the intertwined serpents in almost all its varieties. A very remarkable one occurs in M. Allard's collection of sculptures; in which the dragons forming it have each a man's head in his mouth. The gods of Mexico are frequently pictured fighting with serpents and dragons; and gods, and sometimes men, are represented in conversation with the same loathsome creatures. There is scarcely, indeed, a feature in the mystery of Ophiolatreia which may not be recognised in the Mexican superstitions.

We perceive, therefore, that in the kingdom of Mexico the serpent was sacred, and emblematic of more gods than one: an observation which may be extended to almost every other nation which adored the symbolical serpent. This is a remarkable and valuable fact, and it discovers in Ophiolatreia another feature of its aboriginal character. For it proves the serpent to have been a symbol of intrinsic divinity, and not a mere representative

* Faber.

of peculiar properties which belong to some gods and not to others." *

From what has been presented, it will be seen that the serpent symbol was of general acceptance in America, particularly among the semi-civilised nations; that it entered widely into their symbolic representations, and this significance was essentially the same with that which attached to it among the early nations of. the old continent. Upon the basis, therefore, of the identity which we have observed in the elementary religious conceptions of the Old and New World, and the striking uniformity in their symbolical systems, we feel justified in ascribing to the emblematic Serpent and Egg of Ohio a significance radically the same with that which was assigned to the analogous compound symbol among the primitive nations of the East. This conclusion is further sustained by the character of some of the religious structures of the old continent, in which we find the symbolic serpent and the egg or circle represented on a most gigantic scale. Analogy could probably furnish no more decisive sanction, unless by exhibiting other structures, in which not only a general correspondence, but an absolute identity should exist. Such an identity it would be unreasonable to look for, even in the works of the same people, constructed in accordance with a common design.

It may seem hardly consistent with the caution which should characterize researches of this kind, to hazard the suggestion that the symbolical Serpent and Egg of Ohio are distinctly allusive to the specific notions of cosmogony which prevailed among the nations of the East, for the reason that it is impossible to bring positive collateral proof that such notions were entertained by any of the American nations. The absence of written records and of impartially preserved traditions we have already had ample reason to deplore; and unless further explorations shall present us with unexpected results, the deficiency may always

* Deane:

t. But we must remember that in no respect are men more
cious than in the preservation of their rudimental religious
efs and early conceptions. In the words of a philosophical
stigator—" Of all researches that most effectually aid us to
over the origin of a nation or people whose history is involved
he obscurity of ancient times, none perhaps are attended with
n important results as the analysis of their theological dogmas
their religious practices. To such matters mankind adhere
h the greatest tenacity, which, though modified and corrupted
the revolution of ages, still retain features of their original
struction, when language, arts, sciences and political establish-
ts no longer preserve distinct lineaments of their ancient
stitutions." *

A striking example of the truth of these remarks is furnished
the religion of India, which, to this day, notwithstanding the
olution of time and empire, the destructions of foreign and
civil wars, and the constant addition of allegorical fictions
ore fatal to the primitive system than all the other causes
nbined), still retains its original features, which are easily
ognisable, and which identify it with the religions which pre-
led in monumental Egypt, on the plains of Assyria, in the
lleys of Greece, among the sterner nations around the Caspian,
d among their kindred tribes on the rugged shores of
andinavia.

This tenacity is not less strikingly illustrated in the careful
rpetuation of rites, festivals and scenic representations which
ginated in notions which have long since become obsolete, and
e now forgotten. Very few of the attendants on the annual
ay-day festival, as celebrated a few years back in this country,
d very few of those who have read about the same are aware
at it was only a perpetuation of the vernal solar festival of
aal, and that the garlanded pole was anciently a Phallic emblem.

* McCulloch's American Researches, p. 225.   H

CHAPTER VII.

Egypt as the Home of Serpent Worship—Thoth said to be the founder of Ophiolatreia—Cneph, the Architect of the Universe— Mysteries of Isis—The Isaic Table—Frequency of the Serpent Symbol—Serapis—In the Temples of Luxore, etc.—Discovery at Malta — The Egyptian Basilisk — Mummies — Bracelets— The Caduceus—Temple of Cneph at Elephantina—Thebes—Story of a Priest—Painting in a Tomb at Biban at Malook—Pococke at Raigny.

EGYPT, of all ancient nations the most noted for its idolatry, was in its earliest days the home of the peculiar worship we are contemplating. A learned writer on the subject says "the serpent entered into the Egyptian religion under all his characters—of an Emblem of Divinity, a Charm or Oracle, and a God." Cneph, Thoth and Isis were conspicuous and chief among the gods and goddesses thus symbolized, though he is said to have entered more or less into the symbolical worship of all the gods.

Sanchoniathon describes Thoth as the founder of Serpent Worship in Egypt, and he is generally regarded as the planter of the earliest colonies in Phœnicia and Egypt after the Deluge. He has been called the Reformer of the Religions of Egypt, and Deane says: "He taught the Egyptians (or rather that part of his colony which was settled in Egypt) a religion, which, partaking of Zabaism and Ophiolatreia, had some mixture also of primeval truth. The Divine Spirit he denominated Cneph, and described him as the Original, Eternal Spirit, pervading all creation, whose symbol was a serpent."

Cneph was called by the priests the architect of the universe, and has been represented as a serpent with an egg in his mouth; the serpent being his hieroglyphical emblem, and the egg setting forth the mundane elements as proceeding from him.

After his death Thoth was, in return for services rendered to the people, made a god of—the god of health, or of healing, and so became the prototype of Æsculapius. His learning appears to have been great, and he instructed the people in astronomy, morals, hieroglyphics and letters. He is generally represented leaning upon a knotted stick which has around it a serpent.

The mysteries of the worship of Isis abounded in allusions to the serpent, and Montfaucon says that the Isaic table, a plate of brass overlaid with brass enamel; intermixed with plates of silver, which described the mysteries, was charged with serpents in every part as emblems of the goddess. The particular serpent thus employed was that small one well known as the instrument used in her suicide by the celebrated Cleopatra, the asp. This creature is pictured and carved on the priestly robes, the tiaras of the kings, the image of the goddess. The British Museum possesses a head of this divinity wearing a coronet of them. Not only so, the living reptiles were kept in her temple and were supposed to sanctify the offerings by crawling about amongst them.

As we have said the serpent entered largely into the symbolical worship of all the Egyptian deities, and Cneph, Thoth and Isis can only be regarded as three of the chief.

Deane says there is scarcely an Egyptian deity which is not occasionally symbolized by it. Several of these deities are represented with their proper heads terminating in serpents' bodies. In Montfaucon, vol. 2, plate 207, there is an engraving of Serapis with a human head and serpentine tail. Two other minor gods are also represented, the one by a serpent with a bull's head, the other by a serpent with the radiated head of the lion. The second of these, which Montfaucon supposes to be an image of Apis, is bored through the middle: probably with a design to hang about the neck, as they did many other small figures of gods, by way of ornament or charms.

The figure of Serapis encircled by serpents is found on tombs.
The appearance of serpents on tombs was very general. On an
urn of Egnatius, Nicephoras, and of Herbasia Clymene, engraved
in Montfaucon, vol. 5, a young man entwined by a serpent is
described as falling headlong to the ground. In the urn of
Herbasia Clymene the corners are ornamented with figures of
serpents. It is a singular coincidence that the creature by whom
it is believed came death into the world should be consecrated by
the earliest heathen idolaters to the receptacles of the dead. It
is remarkable also that Serapis was supposed by the Egyptians
to have dominion over evil demons, or in other words was the
same as Plato or Satan.''

On some of the Egyptian temples the serpent has been conspicuously figured as an emblem consecrated to the Divine
service. Thus it is found at Luxore, Komombu, Dendara,
Apollinopolis and Esnay. The Pamphylian obelisk also bears
it many times—fifty-two it is said—and according to Pococke
each of the pillars of the temple of Gava has it twice sculptured.

All writers on the subject have noticed the variations of form
under which the serpent has appeared on Egyptian monuments,
and have laid stress upon it as indicating the great consideration
in which he was held. There is little to be wondered at in this
when we remember that he was regarded as symbolical of divine
wisdom, power, and creative energy; of immortality and regeneration, from the shedding of his own skin; and of eternity, when
represented in the act of biting his own tail.

One writer says the world was represented by a circle, inter-
sected by two diameters perpendicular to each other, which
diameters, according to Eusebius, were serpents. Jablonski says
the circumference only, was a serpent.

Kircher says that the elements (or rather what were so considered in ancient times) were represented by serpents. Earth

was symbolized by a prostrate two-horned snake; water, by a serpent moving in an undulated manner; air, by an erect serpent in the act of hissing; fire, by an asp standing on its tail and bearing upon his head a globe. " From these hieroglyphics," remarks Deane, " It is clear that the serpent was the most expressive symbol of divinity with the Egyptians."

An engraving in Montfaucon, vol. 2, p. 237, calls for notice here, as illustrating the great extent to which the veneration of the serpent once prevailed in Egypt. In the year 1694, in an old wall of Malta, was discovered a plate of gold, supposed to have been concealed there by its possessors at a time when everything idolatrous was destroyed as abominable. Montfaucon says: " This plate was rolled up in a golden casket; it consists of two long rows which contain a very great number of Egyptian deities, most of which have the head of some beast or bird. Many serpents are also seen intermixed, the arms and legs of the gods terminating in serpents' tails. The first figure has upon its back a long shell with a serpent upon it; in each row there is a serpent extended upon an altar. Among the figures of the sacred row there is seen an Isis of tolerably good form. This same plate, no doubt, contains the most profound mysteries of the Egyptian superstition."

It hardly matters where we look in Egypt, this same serpent symbol is found entering into the composition of everything, whether ornamental, useful, or ecclesiastical. The basilisk, the most venomous of all snakes, and so regarded as the king of the ecies and named after the oracular god of Canaan OB or OUB, is represented on coins with rays upon his head like a crown; around the coin was inscribed " Agathodæmon." The emperor Nero in the " madness of his vanity," it is said, caused a number of such coins to be struck with the inscription " The New Agathodæmon," meaning himself.

The Egyptians held basilisks in such veneration that they made images of them in gold and consecrated and placed them in the temples of their gods.   Bryant thinks that they were the same as the Thermuthis, or deadly asp.   These creatures the Egyptian priests are said to have preserved by digging holes for them in the corners of their temples, and it was a part of their superstition to believe that whosoever was accidentally bitten by them was divinely favoured.*

Deane further mentions that the serpent is sometimes found sculptured, and attached to the breasts of mummies; but whether with a view to talismanic security, or as indicative of the priest-hood of Isis, is doubtful.   A female mummy, opened by M. Passalacqua at Paris some years ago, was adorned with a neck-lace of serpents carved in stone.

Bracelets, in the form of serpents, were worn by the Grecian women in the time of Clemens Alexdrinus, who thus reproves the fashion:—" The women are not ashamed to place about them the most manifold symbols of the evil one; for as the serpent de-ceived Eve, so the golden trinket in the fashion of a serpent misleads the women." The children also wore chaplets of the same kind.

We must not omit to notice the Caduceus, which forms, it is said, one of the most striking examples of the talismanic serpent. According to Montfaucon, Kirchen and others, the notion that this belonged exclusively to Hermes or Mercury is erroneous, as it can be seen in the hand of Cybele, Minerva Amebis, Hercules Ogmius and the personified constellation Virgo, said by Lucian to have had her symbol in the Pythian priestess.

Variously represented in the main, the Caduceus always preserved the original design of a winged wand entwined by two serpents. It is found sometimes without the wings, but never without the serpents; the varieties consisting chiefly in the

* Gesner, Hist. Anim. p. 54, citing Ælian.

number of folds made by the serpents' bodies round the wand,
and the relative positions of the wings and serpents' heads. It
was regarded as powerful in paralyzing the mind and raising the
dead.

Kirchen says that Caduceus was originally expressed by
the simple figure of a cross, by which its inventor, Thoth, is said
to have symbolized the four elements proceeding from a common
centre.

" Ophiolatreia," says Deane, " had taken such deep root in
Egypt that the serpent was not merely regarded as an emblem of
divinity, but even held in estimation as the instrument of an
oracle. The priests of the temple of Isis had a silver image of a
serpent so constructed as to enable a person in attendance to
move its head without being observed by the supplicating votary.

" But Egyptian superstition was not contented with worshipping divinity through its emblem the serpent. The senseless
idolator soon bowed before the symbol itself, and worshipped this
reptile, the representative of man's energy, as a god."

In addition to the temple of the great serpent-god Cneph at
Elephantina, there was a renowned one of Jupiter at Thebes,
where the practice of Ophiolatreia was carried to a great length.
Herodotus writes: " At Thebes there are two serpents, by no
means injurious to men; small in size, having two horns springing up from the top of the head. They bury these when dead in
the temple of Jupiter: for they say that they are sacred to that
god." Ælian says: " In the time of Ptolemy Euergetes, a very
large serpent was kept in the temple of Æsculapius at Alexandria;
and in another place a live one of great magnitude was kept and
adored with divine honours; the name of this place he called
Melité." He gives the following story:—" This serpent had
priests and ministers, a table and a bowl. The priests every day
carried into the sacred chamber a cake made of flour and honey
and then retired. Returning the next day they always found the

bowl empty. On one occasion, one of the priests, being extremely anxious to see the sacred serpent, went in alone, and having deposited the cake retired. When the serpent had ascended the table to his feast, the priest came in, throwing open the door with great violence: upon which the serpent departed with great indignation. But the priest was shortly after seized with a mental malady, and, having confessed his crime, became dumb and wasted away until he died.''

In Hewart's tables of Egyptian hieroglyphics we see a priest offering adoration to a serpent. The same occurs on the Isiac table.

"In a tomb at Biban, at Malook, is a beautiful painting descriptive of the rites of Ophiolatreia. The officiating priest is represented with a sword in his hand, and three headless victims are kneeling before an immense serpent. Isis is seen sitting under the arch made by the serpent's body, and the sacred asp, with a human face, is behind her seated on the serpent's tail. This picture proves that the serpent was propitiated by human victims.'' *

It is noteworthy that in Egypt as in Phœnicia and other places serpent worship was not immediately destroyed by the advance of Christianity. The Gnostics united it with the religion of the cross, and a quotation from Bishop Pococke will, just here, be most appropriate and interesting.

" We came to Raigny, where the religious sheikh of the famous Heredy was at the side of the river to meet us. He went with us to the grotto of the serpent that has been so much talked of under the name of the Sheikh Heredy, of which I shall give you a particular account, in order to show the folly, credulity, and superstition of these people; for the Christians have faith in it as well as the Turks. We went ascending between the rocky mountain for half a mile, and came to a part where the valley opens wider. On the right is a mosque, built with a dome over it, against the side of the rock, like a sheikh's burial-place. In it there is a large cleft in the rock out of which they say the serpent comes. There is a tomb in the mosque, in the Turkish manner, that they say is the tomb of Heredy, which would make one imagine that one of their saints is buried there, and that they suppose his soul may be in the serpent, for I observed that they went and kissed the tomb with much devotion and said their prayers at it. Opposite to this cleft there is another, which they say is the tomb of Ogli Hassan, that is of Hassan, the son of Heredy; there are two other clefts which they say are inhabited by saints or angels. The sheikh told me there were two of these serpents, but the common notion is that there is only one. He said it had been there ever since the time of Mahomet. The shape of it is like that of other serpents of the harmless breed. He comes out only during the four summer months, and it is said that they sacrifice to it. This the sheikh denied, and affirmed they only brought lambs, sheep, and money to buy oil for the lamps—but I saw much blood and entrails of beasts lately killed before the door.

"The stories are so ridiculous that they ought not to be repeated, if it were not to give an instance of their idolatry in those parts in this respect, though the Mahometan religion seems to be very far from it in other things. They say the virtue of this serpent is to cure all diseases of those who go to it.

"They are also full of a story, that when a number of women go there once a year, he passes by and looks on them, and goes and twines about the neck of the most beautiful.

"I was surprised to hear a grave and sensible Christian say that he always cured any distempers, but that worse followed. And some really believe that he works miracles, and say it is the devil mentioned in Tobit, whom the angel Gabriel drove into the utmost parts of Egypt."

The bishop is of opinion (in which he is joined by others) that

CHAPTER VIII.

Derivation of the name "Europe"—Greece colonized by Ophites—
Numerous Traces of the Serpent in Greece—Worship of Bacchus—
Story of Ericthonius—Banquets of the Bacchants—Minerva—
Armour of Agamemnon—Serpents at Epidaurus—Story of the
pestilence in Rome—Delphi—Mahomet at Atmeidan.

BRYANT and Faber both derive the name of "Europe"
from "Aur-ab, the solar serpent." "Whether this be
correct or not," says Deane, "it is certain that Ophiolatreia
prevailed in this quarter of the globe at the earliest period of
idolatry. The first inhabitants of Europe are said to have been
the offspring of a woman, partly of the human and partly of the
dracontic figure, a tradition which alludes to their Ophite origin.

"Of the countries of Europe, Greece was first colonized by
Ophites, but at separate times, both from Egypt and Phœnicia;
and it is a question of some doubt, though perhaps of little
importance, whether the leader of the first colony, the celebrated
Cadmus, was a Phœnician or an Egyptian. Bochart has shown
that Cadmus was the leader of the Canaanites who fled before
the arms of the victorious Joshua; and Bryant has proved that
he was an Egyptian, identical with Thoth. But as mere names
of individuals are of no importance, when all agree that the
same superstition existed contemporaneously in the two countries,
and since Thoth is declared by Sanchoniathan to have been the
father of the Phœnician as well as Egyptian Ophiolatreia; we
may endeavour without presumption to reconcile the opinions of
these learned authors by assuming each to be right in his own
line of argument."

In Greece there are numerous traces of the worship of the
serpent—it was so common indeed at one time that Justin Martyr
declared the people introduced it into the mysteries of all their

gods. In the mysteries and excesses of Bacchus it is well-known, of course, to have played a conspicuous part. The people bore them entwined upon their heads, and carrying them in their hands, swung them about crying aloud, " enia, enia." The sign of the Bacchic ceremonies was a consecrated serpent, and in the processions a troop of virgins of noble family carried the reptile with golden baskets containing sesamum, honey cakes and grains of salt, articles all specially connected with serpent worship. The first may be seen in the British Museum, in the hands of priests kneeling before the sacred serpent of Egypt. Honey cakes, according to Herodotus, were presented once a month as food to the sacred serpent in the Acropolis at Athens.

The most remarkable feature of all in the Bacchic orgies is said to have been the mystic serpent. " The mystery of religion was throughout the world concealed in a chest or box. As the Israelites had their sacred ark, every nation upon earth had some holy receptacle for sacred things and symbols. The story of Ericthonius is illustrative of this remark. He was the fourth King of Athens, and his body terminated in the tails of serpents, instead of legs. He was placed by Minerva in a basket, which she gave to the daughter of Cecrops, with strict injunctions not to open it. Here we have a fable made out of the simple fact of the mysterious basket, in which the sacred serpent was carried at the orgies of Bacchus. The whole legend relates to Ophiolatreia. In accordance with the general practice, the worshippers of Bacchus carried in their consecrated baskets or chests the Mystery of their God, together with the offerings." *.

At the banquets of the Bacchantes, or rather, after them, it was usual to carry round a cup, which was called the "cup of the good dæmon." The symbol of this dæmon was a serpent, as seen on the medals of the town of Dionysopolis in Thrace. On one side were the heads of Gordian and Serapis on the other a coiled serpent.

* Deane.

The serpent was mixed up to a considerable extent with the worship of many other of the Grecian deities. The statues, by Phidias, of Minerva, represent her as decorated with this emblem. In ancient medals, as shown by Montfaucon, she sometimes holds a caduceus in her right hand; at other times she has a staff around which a serpent is twisted, and at others, a large serpent appears going in front of her; while she is sometimes seen with her crest composed of a serpent. It is remarkable too, that in the Acropolis at Athens was kept a live serpent who was generally considered the guardian of the place, and Athens was a city specially consecrated to Minerva.

Examples of Grecian Ophiolatreia might easily be multiplied to a considerable extent, but we have space for little more than a brief glance. It is known that upon the walls of Athens was a sculptured head of Medusa, whose hair was intertwined with snakes, and in the temple at Tega was a similar figure which was supposed to possess talismanic power to preserve or destroy. The print in Montfaucon represents the face of Medusa as mild and beautiful, but the serpents as threatening and terrible. There is a story current, that a priestess going into a sanctuary of Minerva in the dead of the night, saw a vision of that goddess, who held up her mantle upon which was impressed a Medusa's head, and that the sight of this fearful object instantaneously converted the intruder into stone.

The armour of Agamemnon, king of Argos, was ornamented with a three-headed serpent; Menelaus, king of Sparta, had one on his shield, and the Spartan people, with the Athenians, affirmed they were of serpentine origin and called themselves. *ophiogenæ.*

At Epidaurus, according to Pausanias, live serpents were kept and fed regularly by servants, who, on account of religious awe, were fearful of approaching the sacred reptiles which in them-selves were of the most harmless character. The statue of Æsculapius, at this temple, represented him resting one hand upon the head of a serpent, while his sister, Hygeia, had one twisted about her. It is reported that the god Æsculapius was conveyed by a woman named Nicagora, the wife of Echetimus, to Sicyon under the form of a serpent.

Livy, Ovid, Florus, Valerius Maximus, and Aurelius Victor, relate that a pestilence of a violent and fatal character once broke out in Rome, and that the oracle of Delphi advised an embassy to Epidaurus to fetch the god Æsculapius. This advice was taken, and a company of eleven were sent with the humble suppli-cations of the senate and people of Rome. While they were gazing at the statue of the god, a serpent, "venerable, not horrible," say these authors, which rarely appeared but when he intended to confer some extraordinary benefit, glided from his lurking place, and having passed through the city went directly to the Roman vessel and coiled himself up in the berth of Ogul-nius the principal ambassador. Setting sail with the god, they duly arrived off Antium, when the serpent leaped into the sea, and swam to the nearest temple of Apollo, and after a few days returned. But when they entered the Tiber, he leaped upon an island, and disappeared. Here the Romans erected a temple to him in the shape of a ship, and the plague was stayed with won-derful celerity.

Delphi appears to have been the principal stronghold of ser-pent worship in Greece. Strabo says its original name was Pytho—derived from the serpent Python, slain there by Apollo. From this story Heinsius concludes that the god Apollo was first worshipped at Delphi, under the symbol of a serpent. It is known that the public assemblies at Delphi were called Pythia; these were originally intended for the adoration of the Python

In Gibbon and the *Annales Turcici* we have interesting matter about the serpentine column. The former says it was taken from Delphi to Constantinople by the founder of the latter city and set up on a pillar in the Hippodrome. Montfaucon, however, thinks that Constantine only caused a similar column to be made, and that the original remained in its place. Deane says, "this celebrated relic of Ophiolatreia is still to be seen in the same place, where it was set up by Constantine, but one of the serpent's heads is mutilated."

From the *Annales* we get the following explanation of this inquiry. "When Mahomet came to Atmeidan he saw there a stone column, on which was placed a three-headed brazen serpent. Looking at it, he asked, 'What idol is that?' and, at the same time, hurling his iron mace with great force knocked off the lower jaw of one of the serpent's heads. Upon which, immediately, a great number of serpents began to be seen in the city. Whereupon some advised him to leave that serpent alone from henceforth, since through that image it happened that there were no serpents in the city. Wherefore that column remains to this day. And although in consequence of the lower jaw of the brazen serpent being struck off, some serpents do come into the city, yet they do no harm to no one."

Commenting upon this story Deane remarks—"This traditionary legend, preserved by Leunclavius, marks the stronghold which Ophiolatreia must have taken upon the minds of the people of Constantinople, so as to cause this story to be handed down to so late an era as the seventeenth century. Among the Greeks who resorted to Constantinople were many idolators of the old religion, who would wilfully transmit any legend favourable to their own superstition. Hence, probably, the charm mentioned above, was attached by them to the Delphic serpent on the column in the Hippodrome, and revived (after the partial mutilation of the figure) by their descendants, the common people, who are always the last in every country to forego an ancient super- stition. Among the common people of Constantinople, there were always many more Pagans than Christians at heart. With the Christian religion, therefore, which they professed, would be mingled many of the pagan traditions which were attached to the monuments of antiquity that adorned Byzantium, or were im- ported into Constantinople.

CHAPTER IX.

*Ophiolatreia in Britain—The Druids—Adders—Poem of Taliessin
—The Goddess Ceridwen—A Bardic Poem—Snake Stones—The
Anguinum—Execution of a Roman Knight—Remains of the
Serpent-temple at Abury—Serpent vestiges in Ireland of great
rarity—St. Patrick.*

IT will probably be a matter of surprise to many, but it is
a fact that even in Britain in ancient times Ophiolatreia
largely prevailed. Deane says: " Our British ancestors, under
the tuition of the venerable Druids, were not only worshippers of
the solar deity, symbolized by the serpent, but held the serpent,
independent of his relation to the sun, in peculiar veneration
Cut off from all intercourse with the civilized world, partly by
their remoteness and partly by their national character, the
Britons retained their primitive idolatry long after it had yielded
in the neighbouring countries to the polytheistic corruptions of
Greece and Egypt.   In process of time, however, the gods of the
Gaulish Druids penetrated into the sacred mythology of the
British and furnished personifications for the different attributes
of the dracontic god Hu.   This deity was called " The Dragon
Ruler of the World " and his car was drawn by serpents.   His
priests in accommodation with the general custom of the Ophite
god, were called after him " Adders." *

In a poem of Taliessin, translated by Davies, in his Appendix
No. 6, is the following enumeration of a Druid's titles :—

> "I am a Druid; I am an architect ; I am a prophet ;
>   I am a serpent" (Gnadr).

From the word " Gnadr " is derived " adder," the name of a
species of snake. Gnadr was probably pronounced like " adder "
with a nasal aspirate.

The mythology of the Druids contained also a goddess
" Ceridwen," whose car was drawn by serpents. It is conjectured

* Davies' Mythol. of Druids.

that this was the Grecian "Ceres;" and not without reason, for the interesting intercourse between the British and Gaulish Druids introduced into the purer religion of the former many of the corruptions ingrafted upon that of the latter by the Greeks and Romans. The Druids of Gaul had among them many divinities corresponding with those of Greece and Rome. They worshipped Ogmius (a compound deity between Hercules and Mercury), and after him, Apollo, Mars, Jupiter, and Minerva, or deities resembling them. Of these they made images; whereas hitherto the only image in the British worship was the great wicker idol into which they thrust human victims designed to be burnt as an expiatory sacrifice for the sins of some chieftain.

The following translation of a Bardic poem, descriptive of one of their religious rites, identifies the superstition of the British Druids with the aboriginal Ophiolatreia, as expressed in the mysteries of Isis in Egypt. The poem is entitled "the Elegy of Uther Pendragon;" that is, of Uther, "The Dragon's Head;" and it is not a little remarkable that the word "Draig" in the British language signifies, at the same time, a fiery serpent, a dragon, and the Supreme God." *

In the second part of this poem is the following sacrificial rites of Uther Pendragon:—

"With solemn festivity round the two lakes;
    With the lake next my side;
    With my side moving round the sanctuary;
    While the sanctuary is earnestly invoking
    The Gliding King, before whom the Fair One
    Retreats upon the veil that covers the huge stones;
    Whilst the Dragon moves round over
    The places which contain vessels
    Of drink offering;
    Whilst the drink offering is in the Golden Horns;
    Whilst the golden horns are in the hand;
    Whilst the knife is upon the chief victim,
    Sincerely I implore thee, O victorious Bell, etc., etc."

* Owen's Dict. Art. Draig.

I

This is a most minute and interesting account of the religious rites of the Druids, proving in clear terms their addiction to Ophiolatreia: for we have not only the history of the "Gliding King," who pursues "The Fair One," depicted upon "the veil which covers the huge stones "—a history which reminds us most forcibly of the events in Paradise, under a poetic garb; but we have, likewise, beneath that veil, within the sacred circle of "the huge stones," the "Great Dragon, a Living Serpent," moving round the places which contain the vessels of drink-offering; or in other words, moving round the altar stone in the same manner as the serpent in the Isiac mysteries passed about the sacred vessels containing the offerings.

The Golden Horns which contained the drink offerings were very probably of the same kind as that found in Tundera, in Denmark.

The sanctity of the serpent showed itself in another very curious part of the superstition of the British Druids, namely, in that which related to the formation and virtues of the celebrated *anguinum*, as it is called by Pliny, or *gleinen nadroeth*, that is, "snake-stones," as they were called by the Britons." Sir R. C. Hoare in his *Modern Wiltshire*, Hundred of Amesbury, gives an engraving of one, and says: "This is a head of imperfect vitrification representing two circular lines of opaque skylight and white, which seem to represent a snake twined round a centre which is perforated." Mr. Lhwyd, the Welsh antiquary, writing to Ralph Thornley says:—"I am fully satisfied that they were amulets of the Druids. I have seen one of them that had nine small snakes upon it. There are others that have one or two or more snakes."

A story comes to us, on Roman authority (that of Pliny), that a knight entering a court of justice wearing an anguinum about his neck was ordered by Claudius to be put to death, it being believed that the influence would improperly wrest judgment in his favour.

Of this anguinum (a word derived from *anguis*, a snake) Pliny says: " An infinite number of snakes, entwined together in the heat of summer, roll themselves into a mass, and from the saliva of their jaws and the froth of their bodies is engendered an egg, which is called ' anguinum.' By the violent hissing of the serpents the egg is forced into the air, and the Druid destined to secure it, must catch it in his sacred vest before it reaches the ground.''

Information relative to the prevalence of this superstition in England will be found in Davies' *Myths of the Druids*, Camden's *Britannia*, and Borlase's *Cornwall*.

Perhaps the most remarkable of all British relics of this worship are to be found on the hills overlooking the village of Abury, in the county of Wiltshire. There, twenty-six miles from the celebrated ruins of Stonehenge, are to be found the remains of a great Serpentine Temple—one of the most imposing, as it certainly is one of the most interesting, monuments of the British Islands. It was first accurately described by Dr. Stukeley in 1793 in his celebrated work entitled *Abury, a Temple of the British Druids*. It was afterwards carefully examined by Sir R. C. Hoare and an account published in his elaborate work *Ancient Wiltshire*. Dr. Stukeley was the first to detect the design of the structure and his conclusions have been sustained by the observations of every antiquary who has succeeded him.

The temple of Abury consisted originally of a grand circumvallation of earth 1,400 feet in diameter, enclosing an area of upwards of twenty-two acres. It has an inner ditch and the height of the embankment, measuring from the bottom of the

ditch, is seventeen feet.   It is quite regular, though not an exact
circle in form, and has four entrances at equal distances apart,
though nearly at right angles to each other.   Within this grand
circle were originally two double or concentric circles composed
of massive upright stones: a row of large stones, one hundred in
number, was placed upon the inner brow of the ditch.   Extend-
ing upon either hand from this grand central structure were
parallel lines of huge upright stones, constituting, upon each side,
avenues upwards of a mile in length.   These formed the body
of the serpent.   Each avenue consisted of two hundred stones.
·The head of the serpent was represented by an oval structure consisting of two concentric lines of upright stones; the outer line
containing forty, the inner eighteen stones.   This head rests upon
an eminence known as Overton, or Hakpen Hill, from which is
commanded a view of the entire structure, winding back for more
than two miles to the point of the tail, towards Bekhampton.

   Hakpen in the old British dialects signifies *Hak*, serpent, and
pen, head, *i.e.*, Head of the Serpent. " To our name of *Hakpen*,"
says Stukeley, " alludes *ochim*, called ' doleful creatures ' in our
translation."   Isa (13 v. 21), speaking of the desolation of
Babylon, says: Wild beasts of the desert shall lie there, and
their houses shall be full of *ochim*, and owls shall dwell there,
and satyrs shall dance there."   St. Jerome translates it " serpents."   The Arabians call a serpent *Haie*, and wood-serpents
Hageshin; and thence our *Hakpen*; *Pen* is " head " in British.

   " That the votaries of Ophiolatreia penetrated into every part
of Britain is probable from the vestiges of some such idolatry
even now to be found in Scotland and the western isles.   Several
obelisks remain in the vicinity of Aberdeen, Dundee and Perth,
upon which appear devices strongly indicative of Ophiolatreia.
They are engraved in Gordon's *Itinerarium Septentrionale*.   The
serpent is a frequent and conspicuous hieroglyphic.   From the

Runic characters traced upon some of these stones it is conjectured that they were erected by the Danes.   Such might
have been the case; but the Danes themselves were a sect of
Ophites, and had not the people of the country been Ophites also,
they might not have suffered these monuments to remain.'' *

Remains indicating the presence of Serpent Worship in
Ireland are extremely scarce, but we must remember the story
prevalent in the country, accepted as truthful by a large majority
of its inhabitants, that St. Patrick banished all snakes from
Ireland by his prayers.   After all, this may mean nothing more
than that by his preaching he overturned and uprooted the
superstitious practices of the serpent worshippers of his times.

* Moor's Hindu Pantheon 342.

CHAPTER X.

India conspicuous in the history of Serpent Worship—Nagpur—
Confessions of a Snake Worshipper—The gardeners of Guzerat—
Cottages for Snakes at Calicut—The Feast of Serpents—The Deity
Hari—Garuda—The Snake as an emblem of immortality.

IN the course of this work we have had occasion frequently to
allude to India as the home of the peculiar worship before
us, and perhaps that country. may fairly be placed side by side
with Egypt for the multitude of illustrations it affords of what
we are seeking to elucidate.

Mr. Rivett-Carnac, from whose paper in the journal of the
Bengal Asiatic Society we have already quoted, says:—" The
palace of the Bhonslahs at Benares brings me to Nágpúr, where,
many years ago, I commenced to make, with but small success,
some rough notes on Serpent Worship. Looking up some old
sketches, I find that the Mahádeo in the oldest temples at Nágpúr is surmounted by the Nág as at Benares. And in the old
temple near the palace of the Nágpúr, or city of the Nág or
cobra, is a five-headed snake, elaborately coiled. The Bhonslahs
apparently took the many-coiled Nág with them to Benares. A
similar representation of the Nág is found in the temple near the
Itwarah gate at Nágpúr. Here again the Nág or cobra is certainly worshipped at Mahádeo or the phallus, and there are
certain obvious points connected with the position assumed by
the cobra when excited and the expansion of the hood, which
suggest the reason for this snake in particular being adopted as
a representation of the phallus and an emblem of Siva.

" The worship of the snake is very common in the old Nágpúr
Province where, especially among the lower class, the votaries of
Siva or Nág Bhushan, ' he who wears snakes as his ornaments,'
are numerous. It is likely enough that the city took its name

from the Nág temple, still to be seen there, and that the river
Nág, perhaps, took its name from the city or temple, and not the
city from the river, as some think.   Certain it is that many of
the Kunbi or cultivating class worship the snake and the snake
only, and that this worship is something more than the ordinary
superstitious awe with which all Hindus regard the snake.   I
find from my notes that one Kunbi whom I questioned in old
days, when I was a Settlement Officer in camp in the Nágpúr
Division, stated that he worshipped the Nág and nothing else;
that he worshipped clay images of the snake, and when he could
afford to pay snake-catchers for a look at a live one, he worshipped the living snake; that if he saw a Nág on the road he
would worship it, and that he believed no Hindu would kill a
Nág or cobra if he knew it were a Nág.   He then gave me the
following list of articles he would use in worshipping the snake,
when he could afford it; and I take it, the list is similar to what
would be used in ordinary Siva Worship.   1—Water.   2—
Gandh, pigment of sandal-wood for the forehead or body.   3—
Cleaned rice.   4—Flowers.   5—Leaves of the Bail tree.   6—
Milk.   7—Curds.   8—A thread or piece of cloth.   9—Red
powder.   10—Saffron.   11—Abir, a powder composed of fragrant
substances.   12—Garlands of flowers.   13—Buttemah or grain
soaked and parched.   14—Jowarri.   15—Five lights.   16—
Sweetmeats.   17—Betel leaves.   18—Cocoa nut.   19—A sum
of money (according to means).   20—Flowers offered by the
suppliant, the palms of the hands being joined.

" All these articles, my informant assured me, were offered to
the snake in regular succession, one after the other, the worshipper repeating the while certain *mantras* or incantations.
Having offered all these gifts, the worshipper prostrates himself
before the snake, and, begging for pardon if he has ever offended
against him, craves that the snake will continue his favour upon
him and protect him from every danger."

In the *Oriental Memoirs* by Forbes, we are told of the
gardeners of Guzerat who would never allow the snakes to be
disturbed, calling them " father,'' " brother,'' and other familiar
and endearing names.   The head gardener paid them religious
honours.   As Deane saye, " here we observe a mixture of the
original Serpent Worship, with the more modern doctrine of
transmigration.''

Still more striking is the information in Purchas's *Pilgrims*,
that a king of Calicut built cottages for live serpents, whom he
tended with peculiar care, and made it a capital crime for any
person in his dominions to destroy a snake.   " The natives,'' he
says, " looked upon serpents as endued with divine spirits.''

Then there is the festival called " The Feast of the Serpents,''
at which every worshipper, in the hope of propitiating the reptiles
during the ensuing year, sets by a portion of his rice for the
hooded snake on the outside of his house.

The deities of India and the wonderful temples and caves, as
those at Salsette and Elephanta, as may be seen in Maurice's
Indian Antiquities, Moor's *Hindu Pantheon*, *The Asiatic Researches*, Faber's *Pagan Idolatry* and numerous other works, are
universally adorned with, or represented by this great symbol.
Thus we have the statue of Jeyne, the Indian Æsculapius,
turbaned by a seven-headed snake; that of Vishnu on a rock in
the Ganges, reposing on a coiled serpent whose numerous folds
form a canopy over the sleeping god; Parus Nauth symbolized
by a serpent; Jagan-Nath worshipped under the form of a seven-
headed dragon.

Hari appears to be one of the titles of Vishnu—that of the
deity in his preserving quality—and his appearance on the rock,
as just mentioned, is thus noticed in Wilkins' *Hitopadesa*:
" Nearly opposite Sultan Ganj, a considerable town in the
province of Bahar, there stands a rock of granite, forming a small

d in the Ganges, known to Europeans by the name of 'the
of Ichangiri,' which is highly worthy of the traveller's notice
the vast number of images carved upon every part of its
ace. Among the rest there is Hari, of a gigantic size, recum-
upon a coiled serpent, whose heads (which are numerous)
artist has contrived to spread into a kind of canopy over the
ing god; and from each of its mouths issues a forked tongue,
ing to threaten instant death to any whom rashness might
apt to disturb him. The whole lies almost clear of the block
which it is hewn. It is finely imagined and is executed with
t skill. The Hindus are taught to believe that at the end
very *Calpa* (creation or formation) all things are absorbed in
Deity, and that in the interval of another creation, he re-
th himself upon the serpent Sesha (duration) who is also
d Ananta (endlessness)."

Moor says Garuda was an animal—half bird, half man—and
the *vahan* or vehicle of Vishnu, also Arun's younger brother.
is sometimes described in the manner that our poets and
ters describe a griffin or a cherub; and he is placed at the
ance of the passes leading to the Hindu garden of Eden, and
e appears in the character of a destroying angel in as far as
esists the approach of serpents, which in most systems of
ical mythology appears to have been the beautiful, deceiving,
uating form that sin originally assumed. Garuda espoused
autiful woman; the tribes of serpents, alarmed thereat, lest
progeny should, inheriting his propensities, overpower them,
d fierce war against him; but he destroyed them all, save
which he placed as an ornament about his neck. In the
hanta cave Garuda is often seen with this appendage; and
e very old gold coins are in existence depicting him with
es or elephants in his talons and beaks. Destroyer of ser-
s, Naganteka, is one of his names.

He was of great use to Krishna in clearing the country round Dwarka (otherwise Dravira) from savage ferocious animals and noxious reptiles. Vishnu had granted to Garuda the power of destroying his as well as Siva's enemies; also generally those guilty of constant uncleanness, unbelievers, dealers in iniquity, ungrateful persons, those who slander their spiritual guides, or defiled their beds; but forbade him to touch a Brahman, whatever was his guilt, as the pain of disobedience would be a scorching pain in his throat, and any attack on a holy or pious person would be followed by a great diminution of strength. By mistake, however, Garuda sometimes seized a priest or a religious man, but was admonished and punished in the first case by the scorching flame, and was unable, even when he had bound him in his den, to hurt the man of piety.* To Rama also, in the war of Lauka, Garuda was eminently useful: in Rama's last conflict with Ravana the latter was not overcome without the aid of Garuda, sent by Vishnu to destroy the serpent-arrows of Ravana. These arrows are called " Sharpa-vana " (in the current dialect *Sarpa* a snake), is corrupted into *Saap* or *Sāmp* and *vana*; an arrow, into *ban*) and had the faculty of separating, between the bow and the object, into many parts, each becoming a serpent. Viswamitra conferred upon Rama the power of transforming his arrows into " Garuda-vanas," they similarly separating themselves into " Garuda's," the terror and destroyer of the *Sarpa*.

Some legends make Garuda the offspring of Kasyapa and Diti. This all-prolific dame laid an egg, which, it was predicted, would preserve her deliverer from some great affliction. After a lapse of five hundred years Garuda sprung from the egg, flew to the abode of Indra, extinguished the fire that surrounded it, conquered its guards, the *devatas*, and bore off the *amrita* (ambrosia), which enabled him to liberate his captive mother. A few drops

* Asiatic Res., vol. 5, p. 514

of this immortal beverage falling on the species of grass called
"Kusa," it became eternally consecrated; and the serpents
greedily licking it up so lacerated their tongues with the sharp
grass that they have ever since remained forked; but the boon
of eternity was ensured to them by their thus partaking of the
immortal fluid.   This cause of snakes having forked tongues is
still, in the tales of India, popularly attributed to the above
greediness; and their supposed immortality may have originated
in some such stories as these; a small portion of *amrita*, as in
the case of Rahu, would ensure them this boon.

In all mythological language the snake is an emblem of
immortality: its endless figure when its tail is inserted in its
mouth, and the annual renewal of its skin and vigour, afford
symbols of continued youth and eternity; and its supposed
medicinal or life-preserving qualities may also have contributed
to the fabled honours of the serpent tribe.   In Hindu mythology
serpents are of universal occurrence and importance; in some
shape or other they abound in all directions; a similar state of
things prevails in Greece and Egypt.   Ingenious and learned
authors attribute this universality of serpent form to the early
and all pervading prevalence of sin, which, in this identical
shape, they tell us, and as indeed we all know, is as old as the
days of our greatest grandmother: thus much as to its age,
when there was but one woman; its prevalence, now there are so
many, this is no place to discuss.

If such writers were to trace the allegories of Sin and Death,
and the end of their empire, they might discover further allusions
to the Christian dispensation in the traditions of the Hindus than
have hitherto been published—Krishna crushing, but not destroying the type of Siva, has often been largely discussed.   Garuda
is also the proverbial, but not the utter destroyer of serpents, for
he spared one, they and their archetype being, in reference to

created beings, eternal. His continual and destined state of war-
fare with serpents, a shape mostly assumed by the enemies of the
virtuous incarnations or deified heroes of the Hindus, is a continued allegory of the conflicts between Vice and Virtue so in-
finitely personified. Garuda, at length, appears the coadjutor of
all virtuous sin-subduing efforts, as the vehicle of the chastening
and triumphant party, and conveys him on the wings of the winds
to the regions of eternal day.

CHAPTER XI.

Mr. Bullock's Exhibition of Objects illustrating Serpent Worship.

UPWARDS of sixty years ago, there was opened at the Egyptian Hall, Piccadilly, what was described as the "Unique Exhibition called Ancient Mexico; collected on the spot in 1823, by the assistance of the Mexican Government, by W. Bullock, F.L.S., &c., &c." The illustration attached to a published description of this collection shows that it contained reproductions of some of the most remarkable of the serpent deities to be found in the temples of the western parts of America, and the following extract will prove interesting to our readers.

" The rattlesnake appears to have been the most general object of worship, veneration, and fear; indeed it occurs in some manner combined with almost every other, and is still found in many of the Indian villages. It remains at Tezcuco, quite perfect at the present time. Broken fragments may be met with in the exterior of the houses in Mexico in several places; the great head placed at the left of the sacrificial stone is cast from one in the corner of the fine building used for the Government Lottery Office, and exposed to the street. It must have belonged to an idol at least seventy feet long, probably in the great temple, and broken and buried at the Conquest. They are generally in a coiled up state, with the tail or rattle on the back, but they vary in their size and position. The finest that is known to exist, I discovered in the deserted part of the Cloister of the Dominican Convent opposite the Palace of the Inquisition. It is coiled up in an irritated erect position, with the jaws extended, and in the act of gorging an elegantly dressed female, who appears in the mouth of the enormous reptile, crushed and lacerated, a disgusting detail withal too horrible for description.

" Turning to a letter from Cortes to Charles V., as given by Humboldt, we read, ' From the square we proceeded to the great temple, but before we entered it we made a circuit through a number of large courts, the smallest of which appeared to me to contain more ground than the great square in Salamanca, with double enclosures built of lime and stone, and the courts paved with large white cut stone, very clean; or, where not paved, they were plastered and polished. When we approached the gate of the great temple, to which the ascent was by a hundred and four-teen steps, and before we had mounted one of them, Montezuma sent down to us six priests and two of his noblemen to carry Cortes up, as they had done their sovereign, which he politely declined. When we had ascended to the summit of the temple, we observed on the platform as we passed the large stone whereon were placed the victims who were to be sacrificed. Here was a great figure which resembled a dragon, and much blood fresh spilt. Cortes then addressing himself to Montezuma requested that he would do him the favour to show us his gods. Montezuma, having first consulted his priests, led us into a tower where there was a kind of saloon. Here were two altars highly adorned, with richly wrought timbers on the roof, and over the altars gigantic figures resembling very fat men. The one on the right was Huitzilopochtli their war god, with a great face and terrible eyes, this figure was entirely covered with gold and jewels, and his body bound with golden serpents, in his right hand he held a bow, and in his left a bundle of arrows. The little idol which stood by him represented his page, and bore a lance and target richly ornamented with gold and jewels. The great idol had round his neck the figures of human heads and hearts made of pure gold and silver, ornamented with precious stones of a blue colour. Before the idol was a pan of incense, with three hearts of human victims which were then burning, mixed with copal.

The whole of that apartment, both walls and floor, was stained with human blood in such quantity as to give a very offensive smell. On the left was the other great figure, with a countenance like a bear, and great shining eyes of the polished substance whereof their mirrors are made. The body of this idol was also covered with jewels. These two deities it was said were brothers; the name of the last was Tezcatepuca, and he was the god of the infernal regions. He presided, according to their notions, over the souls of men. His body was covered with figures representing little devils with tails of serpents, and the walls and pavement of this temple were so besmeared with blood that they gave off a worse odour than all the slaughter-houses of Castille. An offering lay before him of five human hearts. In the summit of the temple, and in a recess the timber of which was highly ornamented, we saw a figure half human and the other half resembling an alligator, inlaid with jewels, and partly covered with a mantle. This idol was said to contain the germ and origin of all created things, and was the god of harvests and fruits. The walls and altars were bestained like the rest, and so offensive that we thought we never could get out soon enough.

"In this place they had a drum of most enormous size, the head of which was made of the skins of large serpents. This instrument when struck resounded with a noise that could be heard to the distance of two leagues, and so doleful that it deserved to be named the music of the infernal regions; and with their horrible sounding horns and trumpets, their great knives for sacrifice, their human victims, and their blood besprinkled altars, I devoted them and all their wickedness to God's vengeance, and thought that the time would never arrive that I should escape from this scene of butchery, horrible smells, and more detestable sights.

"'On the site of the church, called St. Jago el Taltelulco, was a temple, which, we have already observed, was surrounded with

courts as large as the square of Salamanca. At a little distance
from it stood a tower, a true hell or habitation for demons, with
a mouth, resembling that of an enormous monster, wide open,
and ready as it were to devour those who entered. At the door
stood frightful idols; by it was a place for sacrifice, and within,
boilers and pots full of water to dress the flesh of the victims
which were eaten by the priests. The idols were like serpents
and devils, and before them were tables and knives for sacrifice,
the place being covered with the blood which was spilt on those
occasions. The furniture was like that of a butcher's stall, and
I never gave this accursed building any name except that of hell.
Having passed this, we saw great piles of wood, and a reservoir
of water supplied by a pipe from the great aqueduct; and cross-
ing a court we came to another temple, wherein were the tombs
of the Mexican nobility, it was begrimed with soot and blood.
Next to this was another, full of skeletons and piles of bones,
each kept apart, but regularly arranged. In each temple were
idols, and each had also its particular priests, who wore long
vestments of black, their long hair was clotted together, and their
ears lacerated in honour of their gods.' "

Mr. Bullock then proceeds to describe a cast of the great idol
of the goddess of war, which he had brought to England with him.

" This monstrous idol, before which thousands of human
victims were annually sacrificed on the altar is, with its pedestal,
about twelve feet high and four feet wide, it is sculptured out of
one solid piece of grey basalt. Its form is partly human, and
the rest composed of rattlesnakes and the tiger. The head,
enormously wide, seems that of two rattlesnakes united, the fangs
hanging out of the mouth, on which the still palpitating hearts of
the unfortunate victims were rubbed as an act of the most accept-
able oblation. The body is that of a deformed human frame, and
the place of arms supplied by the heads of rattlesnakes placed on

square plinths and united by fringed ornaments.   Round the
waist is a girdle, which was originally covered with gold, and beneath this, reaching nearly to the ground and partly covering its
deformed cloven feet, a drapery entirely composed of wreathed
rattlesnakes which the nations call cohuatlicuye or garments of
serpents, on each side of which is a winged termination of the
feathers of the vulture.   Between the feet, descending from the
body, another wreathed serpent rested its head on the ground, and
the whole composition of this deity is strictly appropriate to the
infernal purpose for which it was used, and with which the per-
sonal ornaments too well accord.   From the neck, spreading over
its deformed breast, is a necklace composed of human hands,
hearts, and skulls—fit emblems of the sanguinary rites daily performed in its honour.

" The death's head and mutilated hands, four of which sur-
round the bosom of the goddess, remind us of the terrible sacrifices of Teoquawhquat, celebrated in the fifteenth century period
of thirteen days after the summer solstice, in honour of the god of
war and his female companion, Teoyamiqui.   The mutilated
hands alternate with the figure of certain vases in which incense
was burnt.   These vases were called Topxicalli, bags in the form
of calabashes.   This idol was sculptured on every side, even beneath where was represented Mictlanteuchtli, the Lord of the
place of the dead; it cannot be doubted, but that it was supported in the air by means of two columns, on which rested the
arms.   According to this whimsical arrangement, the head of the
idol was probably elevated five or six metres above the pavement
of the temple, so that the priests dragging their unfortunate victims to the altar made them pass under the figure of Mictlanteuchtli.   The Viceroy of Mexico transported this monument to
the University which he thought the most proper place to preserve one of the most curious remains of American antiquity.

K

The Professors of the University, monks of the Order of St. Dominic, were unwilling to expose this idol to the sight of the Mexican youth, and caused it to be reburied in one of the passages of the College.   But Mr. Humboldt had it disinterred at the request of the Bishop of Monterey.

" A highly curious specimen of Mexican sculpture is an exceeding hard stone resembling hornstein, a coarse kind of jade, it is a species of compact talc, of most elaborate workmanship, and the bust of a priest, or perhaps of the idol representing the Sun.   The head is crowned with a high mitre-shaped cap, decorated with jewels and feathers, it has long pendant earrings.   The hands are raised, the right sustains something resembling a knotted club, while the left takes hold of a festoon of flowers which descends from the head ; all the other parts are covered with the great rattlesnake, whose enormous head and jaws are on the right side of the figure, while the backs and sides are covered with the scales and rattles of the deadly reptile."

Our prescribed limits are now reached, and we are able to add but little to what has already been advanced exhibiting the widespread prevalence of this singular form of worship.   Again and again has wonderment been expressed that it should ever be possible for a creature so disgusting to become an object of worship, but so it has been, and no age or country seems to have been strange to it.   Very early indeed in history men began to worship a serpent, that brazen one of the Exodus, which Hezekiah destroyed on account of the idolatry into which it led the people. But if that object was put away, the hope that the worship would cease was vain, for it started up amongst the Assyrians, the Chaldeans, the Phœnicians, the Egyptians, and spread into Greece, Esthonia, Finland, Italy, Persia, Hindustan, Ceylon, China, Japan, Burmah, Java, Arabia, Syria, Ethiopia, Britain, Mexico, and Peru.

Such was its extent—wide as the world itself, and vast beyond estimate or description was its influence over the minds of those who came within its reach.   Let the curious reader who would know more, and who would make himself acquainted with the multitudinous forms in which the emblem was depicted, study the works of such writers as Kingsford and Montfaucon, with their numerous and well executed plates, and he will meditate with astonishment upon the singular fascination which this repulsive reptile seems to have exercised over the human mind.   He is said, we know, so to fascinate the victim he is about to seize as his prey that the unhappy creature is deprived of all power of resistance, a fascination no less overwhelming seems to have paralyzed the human mind and caused it to adopt from some cause or other such a repelling reptile as an object of worship.   The spell is broken now, however, and but little remains of what was once so universal, beyond the earth mounds where its temples stood and the half ruined sculptures collected in the museums of civilized countries.

THE END.

Lightning Source UK Ltd.
Milton Keynes UK
UKHW050953150223
417035UK00010B/224